AS Government & Politics

UK Elections & Electoral Reform

Neil Smith

Advanced TopicMaster

2nd Edition

Series editor
Eric Magee

Philip Allan Updates, an imprint of Hodder Education, an Hachette UK company, Market Place, Deddington, Oxfordshire OX15 0SE

Orders

Bookpoint Ltd, 130 Milton Park, Abingdon, Oxfordshire OX14 4SB

tel: 01235 827827

fax: 01235 400401

e-mail: education@bookpoint.co.uk

Lines are open 9.00 a.m.–5.00 p.m., Monday to Saturday, with a 24-hour message answering service. You can also order through the Philip Allan Updates website: www.philipallan.co.uk

ISBN 978-1-4441-2140-7

First printed 2011
Impression number 5 4 3 2 1
Year 2015 2014 2013 2012 2011

Printed in Spain

Hachette UK's policy is to use papers that are natural, renewable and recyclable products and made from wood grown in sustainable forests. The logging and manufacturing processes are expected to conform to the environmental regulations of the country of origin.

P01819

Contents

Contents

Introduction

Over the last 13 years the UK has become obsessed with elections. As well as the usual round of general and European Parliament elections every 4 or 5 years, elections for regional assemblies and mayors have ensured that discussion about how different systems work, and the results of these elections, is rarely out of the media. Throw in the country's first ever referendum on which electoral system should be used to elect MPs, and one can confidently assert that interest in elections and electoral systems has never been greater.

This second edition of *UK Elections & Electoral Reform* adopts a similar approach to its predecessor, in that it focuses on the key issues affecting elections in modern-day democracies, the relative merits of the different electoral systems used in the UK, and the interrelationship between voting behaviour and election campaigns. Where it differs is in a much tighter focus on two areas of UK politics which have received considerable coverage in recent years: the notion of a 'participation crisis' among the electorate; and the growth of participatory, or direct, democratic approaches.

There is extensive coverage of the 2010 general election, as well as analysis and evaluation of the elections which have taken place in London, Scotland, Wales and Northern Ireland and the mayoral contests since the first edition was published in 2007. There is also an appraisal of the effects of 'new social media' and the internet on the 2010 campaign, and a consideration of how far 2010 was the first genuine 'internet election'.

A range of AS-style questions are included at the end of each chapter, reflecting the approaches used by AQA, Edexcel and OCR. Guidance on how to approach these tasks is provided online at **www.hodderplus.co.uk/philipallan** — go to the Government and Politics section.

How effectively do elections promote democracy?

The notion that people are free to participate in the political process and are able to hold their rulers to account is a relatively new one. Today, though, democracy is held to be an ideal for any modern state irrespective of its history, culture or location. Both the invasion of Iraq and the deployment of NATO forces to Afghanistan have been justified on the grounds of establishing and preserving democracy in those two countries. Closer to home, with concerns over 'dodgy dossiers', MPs' expenses, falling turnout, and the workings of the electoral system, increased attention has been paid to the idea that democracy is as much about process as results. This chapter focuses on the relationship between elections and democracy, but also explores the extent to which a participation crisis exists in UK politics and how far it has been redressed.

What is democracy?

The difficulty in answering this question lies in the fact that any definition depends entirely on when it is written or the time to which it is referring. Nowadays, for example, we would commonly associate phrases such as 'popular participation', 'the public interest' or 'political equality' with democracy, and as such we regard it as essentially a good thing.

However, this has not always been the case. In ancient Athens, democracy was more often regarded as something to be avoided. A number of classical scholars wrote at length on the apparent flaws in democracy. Aristotle defined 'rule of the people' as government by the propertyless, uneducated masses, who used power to serve their own ends — that is, to overtax the wealthy.

The influence of the Greek anti-democrats was such that the term 'democracy' did not make a political comeback until the American War of Independence, which ushered in not only a new era of democracy, but also an entirely new form of democracy. Indeed, the modern interpretation can be traced back to Abraham Lincoln's classic reinterpretation of democracy as 'government of the people…by the people…for the people'.

In spite of its widespread use, not every political theorist has agreed that democracy is necessarily a good thing. Up until the nineteenth century, the term was used pejoratively to describe a state of 'mob rule'. An outline of the main arguments over the concept's strengths and weaknesses is provided in Table 1.1.

Table 1.1 Merits and criticisms of democracy

Merits	Criticisms
Social democrats It fosters a sense of community.	*Plato* Some people are not capable of governing themselves.
Locke It enables citizens to check the power of government.	*De Tocqueville* Majority rule ignores the wishes of significant minorities.
Rousseau The ability to make one's own laws makes man truly free.	*Michels* True democracy is impossible to achieve as power always ends up in the hands of a wealthy, well-organised elite.

Democracy is also a 'contested concept', in that there is a range of interpretations of what it actually stands for. The main argument is between supporters of **direct democracy** and those of **representative democracy**, and revolves around the extent of popular participation in the democratic process.

Direct democracy

In this model, citizens participate directly in the government of the state, thus creating genuine government 'by the people'. This idea of mass participation was epitomised by the Athenian model of democracy, where all citizens were expected to participate in decision making.

Representative democracy

This is a restrictive and partial form of democracy, as citizens only participate either at election time or via interest groups, and do not exercise power on their own behalf. However, citizens can control the actions of the executive through regular elections.

The main issues surrounding the concept of **representation** have focused on the questions of who votes, how they vote and for what they vote. Scholars have also disagreed about how one person is supposed to represent another and what elected individuals actually represent. Table 1.2 outlines different theories of representation.

Table 1.2 Theories of representation

Model	Key points
Trustee model	Edmund Burke argued that MPs had a moral duty to take a long-term, national view of issues, and that constituents should have no control over them other than at election time.
Delegate model	MPs are nothing more than a mouthpiece for their constituents. As such, they must vote in Parliament exactly according to constituents' wishes. MPs' own views on a matter are of little consequence.
Mandate model	MPs are not elected on their own merits but simply as representatives of a particular party. Once elected, they have a mandate to ensure that the party's manifesto is implemented. Therefore, they have to support their party at all times, unless it fails to deliver on its manifesto promises.

The most common form of representative democracy in the modern age is often referred to as **liberal democracy**.

Liberal democracy

Modern-day liberal democracies have come to possess most, if not all, of the following characteristics:
- They are representative democracies. Political authority is based on popular consent.
- Popular consent may be given by the whole adult population.
- Elections must be free and fair.
- Open competition must exist between individuals, groups and parties.
- Civil liberties should be protected through the 'rule of law'.
- Individual rights should be protected through the separation of powers.

The two main ways in which liberal democracies work are through **parliamentary systems** and **presidential systems**.

Parliamentary systems

In parliamentary systems (see Figure 1.1), the leader of the government (the prime minister) holds his or her position by virtue of the fact that he or she is the leader of the largest party in the legislature. The leader appoints the members of his or her government largely from the legislature. In the UK, the majority of ministers are elected Members of Parliament, and a relatively small number are appointed members of the House of Lords.

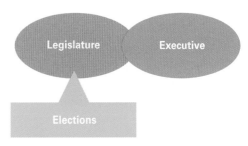

Figure 1.1 Parliamentary democracy

Box 1.1

Does the UK parliamentary system conform to liberal democratic principles?

Yes

- The government consists mostly of elected representatives, and is accountable to the electorate at least once every 5 years.
- All adults over the age of 18 who are on the electoral register are eligible to vote.
- The government is directly accountable to Parliament.
- Voting is conducted in secret, but the process of counting votes is transparent, and candidates have the right to demand a recount or even challenge results in the courts.
- Anyone is free to contest an election so long as he or she is a British, Irish or Commonwealth citizen and can pay a deposit of £500.
- The 2005 Constitutional Reform Act formally separated the judiciary from the executive and legislature.
- The incorporation of the European Convention of Human Rights into UK law in 2000 provided additional protection of individual liberties for UK citizens.

No

- Not all members of the government are accountable to elected representatives. Currently, Lord Strathclyde and Baroness Warsi are the only Cabinet members who sit in the House of Lords, while there are ten further minsters who sit in the Lords. Jonathan Hill and Sir James Sassoon are also unelected ministers, who have been given life peerages to enable them to sit in the Lords.
- The electoral system creates an 'elective dictatorship', which, together with the doctrine of parliamentary sovereignty, can undermine the principle of the rule of law.
- Increasing areas of policy are decided by the European Union, in which the bulk of power rests with the unelected European Commission.
- Some commentators would argue that recent criminal justice legislation, particularly that designed to counter the threat of terrorism, has undermined basic civil liberties.

Presidential systems

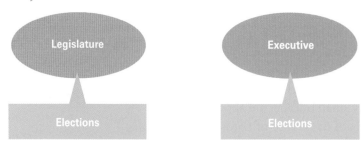

Figure 1.2 Presidential democracy

Presidential systems differ from parliamentary systems in several ways, the most significant being the relationship between the executive and the legislature (see Figure 1.2). Whereas in a parliamentary system the institutions are entwined, presidential systems have a distinct separation of powers. The legislature has the power to reject presidential initiatives, and the president can veto legislative laws. This system of checks and balances is designed to prevent one institution dominating any of the others.

How has the concept of liberal democracy been criticised?

Marxists criticise liberal democracy on the grounds that it is a smokescreen for the continued exploitation of the masses. They argue that it is an integral part of the capitalist system, and is designed to give the impression of democracy while actually placing power in the hands of a wealthy elite. Voting is restricted to infrequent elections, and the range of policies in the political system is limited.

Some Conservatives have also levelled criticisms at UK liberal democracy. In 1976, Lord Hailsham famously described the British system as an 'elective dictatorship'. He feared that the doctrine of parliamentary sovereignty threatened one of the main pillars of the UK constitution: the 'rule of law'. Coupled with the distorting effect of the UK electoral system, this could effectively lead to one-party rule.

How healthy is democracy in the UK?

It has become customary to paint a fairly bleak picture of the state of democracy in the UK at the start of the second decade of the twenty-first century. At the core of this pessimistic view is concern about widespread disengagement with the political process, and a barely-concealed disdain for politicians themselves.

UK democracy is not healthy

Evidence to support this pessimistic view is not difficult to find.

- The system used to elect MPs has come under increasing scrutiny for its inability to fairly translate the views of the electorate into actual seats in the House of Commons.
- Turnout in all forms of elections is depressingly low. Although turnout in 2010 was just over 5% higher than the historic low of 59.4% in 2001, it was some way short of the previous postwar low of 71% in 1997. The figures are even worse for the various second-order elections which take place in the UK:
  - 2009 European Parliament 34.7% (EU average 43%)
  - 2007 Scottish Parliament 51.1%
  - 2007 Welsh Assembly 43.7%
  - 2007 Northern Ireland Assembly 63.5%
  - 2008 London Mayoral elections 45.3%
- Membership of political parties has been in decline since the start of the 1970s. Although the accuracy of membership totals before the 1980s is open to question, a clear trend emerges when you look at the respective memberships of each of the main parties. In 1983, almost 4% of the population were members of the Labour, Conservative or Liberal/Social Democratic parties. By 2005 the figure had fallen to 1.3%. In a submission to the Speaker's Conference (on Parliamentary Representation) in 2009, Dame Jean Roberts highlighted one of the consequences of this decline:

> Increasingly people know fewer people who are a member of a political party. It becomes something very distant, something very remote and something that other people do and I think that is a real danger…that the political class becomes so divorced and distanced from the rest of the population.

In addition, it also has an important impact on a party's ability to raise money. Falling subscriptions forces parties to rely more heavily on individual donors, powerful institutions such as the trade unions, or on loans.

- Activism within the parties has become less prevalent. According to the 2007 Power Report, almost 80% of Conservative Party members spend no time on party business, with the figure for Labour rising throughout the last two decades to approximately 65%.
- The public, on the whole, identify less strongly with political parties. In 1964, over 40% of the population said that they felt a strong identification with a political party, yet by the end of the 1990s less than 15% of respondents felt the same way.

- Surveys of people's attitudes suggest the public does not trust politicians. A survey for Ipsos MORI published in September 2009 found that only 13% of the population trusted politicians to tell the truth, and 16% trusted government ministers to tell the truth.
- After the notorious 'bigotgate' incident between Gordon Brown and pensioner Gillian Duffy in Rochdale, numerous journalists and political commentators used the prime minister's 'private' thoughts on her attitude to immigration as a classic illustration of the 'disconnect' which exists between the voters and the political class. The *Guardian*'s John Harris neatly summarised this disconnect, commenting that Brown represented a 'political class that affects to feel their (voters') pain, but too often holds them in borderline contempt' ('"Bigot" jibe exposes disconnect between politicians and voters', 28 April 2010).
- There is some evidence that dissatisfaction with the main parties has led to an increase in support for extremist parties such as the British National Party. As well as winning seats at local level, in the Greater London Assembly and the European Parliament, the party has bucked the national trend in terms of membership, with this increasing dramatically from 2,200 in 2001 to approximately 14,000 in 2009.

The reasons why democracy in the UK appears to be experiencing something of a participation crisis are varied, but, to a large extent, interlinked (see Figure 1.3).

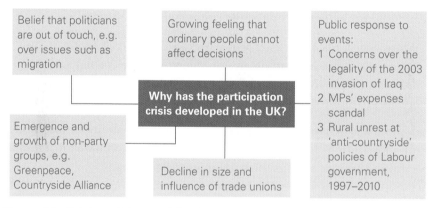

Figure 1.3 Origins of the participation 'crisis' in the UK

UK democracy is healthy

In defiance of this negative prognosis, there is a strong argument to suggest that while people's political behaviour has changed during the last two decades, the extent to which they are active remains considerable.

- Evidence from the Power Inquiry and the 2010 Citizenship Survey indicates that almost half the population engages in some form of voluntary activity at least once per month.
- In the period April to September 2009, 35% of the population engaged in some form of civic activism such as signing a petition, contacting an MP or councillor, or attending a council meeting.
- There has been a sharp rise in membership totals for groups which either pursue an exclusive campaigning agenda, such as Greenpeace, or those which combine campaigning with leisure-time pursuits. Membership of the National Trust, for example, has grown from 278,000 in 1971 to 3,500,000 in 2007. This trend reflects an increased willingness of citizens to actively support single or general campaigns by going on demonstrations and signing petitions.
- Recent years have seen huge demonstrations over issues such as the war in Iraq and the future of the countryside, and mass-participation events such as Live 8.

A Stop the War protest took place as Tony Blair gave evidence to the Chilcot inquiry in January 2010

- There has been a sharp rise in the number of informal political protests. As well as high-profile campaigns by groups such as Fathers4Justice, Plane Stupid, and the fuel protesters in 2000, 2005 and 2007, people are using their power as consumers to make political statements. With increased attention focused on issues such as the environmental, labour, political, ethical and even corporate governance standards that a firm uses, the power of the purse has been directed at companies as diverse as Shell, McDonald's, Starbucks and Focus DIY.

- In a more positive fashion, consumers are more likely to consider political or ethical factors when making financial purchases or regular transactions. Fairtrade goods have probably been the biggest beneficiary of this trend, with sales of all Fairtrade products increasing from £16.7 million in 1998 to £799.0 million in 2009.
- Membership of smaller political parties continues to grow. The British National Party (BNP), the Green Party, the Scottish National Party (SNP) and the United Kingdom Independence Party (UKIP) have all enjoyed quite healthy increases in their memberships.

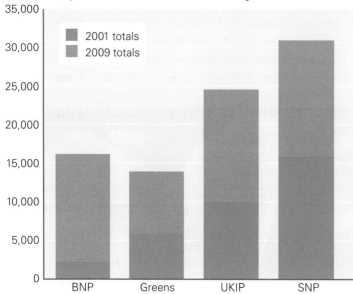

Figure 1.4 Rise in membership totals for smaller UK political parties, 2001–09

Source: House of Commons Library research paper: 'Membership of UK political parties' (2009)

What attempts have been made to enhance democracy in the UK in recent years?

The above evidence suggests that there are two main issues which have to be addressed in order to enhance representative democracy in the UK:
- increasing the extent, nature and depth of participation
- rebuilding trust in the political system

Increasing participation

The bulk of initiatives designed to increase the extent of participation in elections have focused on improving accessibility. The extent to which they have been successful is dealt with in more detail in Chapter 6.

The main political parties have struggled to respond to the membership crisis afflicting each of them in the UK. While there have been short-term increases in membership, particularly in the Labour Party during the mid-1990s, they have not been sustained, nor experienced across the political spectrum.

However, each of the parties has introduced measures designed to increase opportunities for ordinary members to participate in candidate selection and policy making. These have included the use of constituency primaries to select candidates, introducing one-member-one-vote-systems to elect party leaders, and consultations over joining a coalition government in 2010.

The 2006 Power Report provided a comprehensive diagnosis of the problems afflicting representative democracy and prescribed an extensive range of solutions. These included:

- replacing first-past-the-post (FPTP) with single transferable vote (STV) for elections to the House of Commons
- reducing the voting age
- improving political education in schools
- holding more referendums on single issues
- reforming the way parties are funded to make them less dependent on wealthy individual donors

Further recommendations for boosting membership, making parties (and MPs) more representative, and encouraging local activism were provided in the report of the all-party Speaker's Conference on Parliamentary Representation, published in January 2010. Box 1.2 provides a summary of the report's main conclusions.

Box 1.2

Main conclusions of the Speaker's Conference on Parliamentary Representation (2010)

- Parties need to rebuild from the bottom up, developing a culture of strong local activism.
- Parties should place a greater emphasis on personal canvassing.
- Parties should actively recruit members of underrepresented groups.
- They should consider providing matching funds to local parties.

Box 1.2 (continued)

- Parties should review strategies for retaining new members. Local parties should reconsider when and where they meet, and shift emphasis from discussion of procedural matters to more social debates and talks.
- Parties should appoint 'community champions' for women, and other minority groups. Part of their role would be 'talent-spotting' members of these groups within the party or the wider community.
- The teaching of citizenship within schools should be promoted.

Rebuilding trust in the political system

Arguably the biggest challenge facing the political establishment is rebuilding the electorate's trust in and support for the UK's political system. Concern over the decision-making process which led the country into war in Iraq in 2003, limitations on individual freedom under anti-terrorism legislation, alongside damaging scandals such as that over MPs' expenses have undermined public support for politicians and the political system as a whole.

As part of an attempt to restore public trust in the integrity of MPs, Christopher Kelly, chairman of the Committee on Standards in Public Life, made the following recommendations:

- MPs should only be allowed to claim up to £1,450 a month to rent a second home. MPs with constituencies within 20 miles or 60 minutes of Westminster will not be allowed to claim at all.
- No claims will be allowed for cleaning or gardening.
- MPs will be able to employ a maximum of one relative or partner.
- MPs sharing rental accommodation can claim a maximum of one-and-a-third of an MP's accommodation budget.
- MPs have to pay for their journey to Westminster and are not allowed to purchase first-class tickets.
- All claims have to be supported by a receipt. Claims for evening meals are only payable up to £15, and only if the House is sitting beyond 7.30 p.m.
- The Independent Parliamentary Standards Authority was established with 'sole responsibility for processing, validating and paying or rejecting MPs' claims for expenses'.

Recall elections

To augment these measures, the coalition government has proposed giving voters the power to recall MPs, with a special election to be held when demanded by 10% of constituents.

Advocates of using recall elections claim they offer a range of benefits to representative democracy:

- They strengthen the link between constituent and MP, marking a shift from a Burkean model of democracy to one more closely resembling a delegatory model.
- The decision to introduce fixed-term parliaments means that without recall the electorate must wait 5 years to voice its opinions on an MP's performance.
- Ultimately, the threat of recall should focus the MP's mind on his or her approach to parliamentary and constituent business.

Even so, recall elections are not without their flaws:

- Recall elections may be used as a campaigning tool to undermine incumbent MPs in marginal seats.
- Working under the threat of recall might force MPs to 'play safe', and avoid making decisions which might be unpopular in their constituencies.
- In a political system where turnout for by-elections tends to be considerably lower than for general elections, there is no guarantee that recall elections will galvanise interest among the public.
- They could be expensive. By-elections in the UK typically cost approximately £100,000 to administer and the parties have a limit of £100,000 imposed to cover the costs of campaigning. In addition, considerable costs will be incurred managing the recall petition, whether it is successful in triggering a by-election or not.

Conclusion: how effectively do elections promote democracy?

Western governments hold a universal belief that elections confer democratic legitimacy on a state. The evidence for this lies in the prolific use of elections to select representatives, governments and local officials, as well as the emphasis placed on elections in demonstrating how far countries in the developing world have moved towards democratic status. However, the extent to which elections are guaranteed to promote democracy is contested.

Elections do not promote democracy effectively

Plurality systems, such as FPTP, do not require an overall majority, and thus cannot claim to represent the wishes of the country as a whole. In the UK this system has, on two occasions, produced a government which did not even achieve a simple majority of votes nationally, in 1951 and February 1974. The result of the 2010 general election produced a coalition government which has developed new rules for dissolving Parliament in order to keep it in power for the full term of 5 years. In this sense, elections in the UK only serve to confirm the power of the elites, and are not concerned with ensuring popular control of the government.

In addition, the 'winner takes all' nature of the UK's electoral system encourages parties to offer a narrow range of policies, designed to appeal to the broadest spectrum of voters. As a consequence, this denies voters a real choice between competing visions at election time. The main parties' approach to the economy is a good example of this problem. While emphasising different aspects of their policies, all three parties take a market-driven approach, offering a small degree of regulation to ameliorate the worst excesses of capitalism.

Even proportional systems can struggle to assert their democratic credentials, as they tend to produce coalition governments, whose survival is dependent on post-election deals being done behind closed doors. The fate of these governments can also rest on the whims of small coalition partners, such as Plaid Cymru in Wales, which joined Labour in a 'One Wales' coalition in 2007. Elections held using proportional representation limit the ability of the electorate to get rid of unpopular governments, and, instead, pass the power of government formation to party elites. After the 2007 Welsh Assembly elections, it took 1 month to form a government, and during that period two very different-looking governments could have been formed. While the party managers of Labour and Plaid Cymru were able to reach an agreement on their 'One Wales' programme, the leaders of the Liberal Democrats, Conservatives

'One Wales' coalition partners in the Welsh National Assembly: Plaid Cymru leader and Deputy First Minister Ieuan Wyn Jones (left) and Labour leader and First Minister Rhodri Morgan (right)

and Plaid Cymru came close to creating a 'rainbow coalition'. The power to decide on the formation of a government was thus in the hands of the parties rather than the electorate.

Elections also fail to perform a key democratic role as they are held so infrequently. Most liberal democratic states' primary claim to democratic status is their commitment to holding regular parliamentary or presidential elections. However, in the period between elections, the wishes of most citizens are ignored.

Declining turnout in general elections, and low turnout in second-order elections, perhaps indicates a lack of public confidence in the ability of elections to promote democracy. This is almost certainly related to the decline in membership of, and lack of activism within, the main political parties. It suggests that elections simply legitimise political control by a narrow elite, and are not concerned with allowing ordinary people to participate in the decision-making process.

Elections do promote democracy effectively

Focusing on elections as the sole barometer of the UK's political health can present an overly negative view of the state of democracy, as it ignores the many other features of a democratic society. The extent of non-party political activity led the Power Report to refer to the existence of an 'apathy myth'.

Elections in liberal democracies provide choice between competing ideas and personnel. This choice is evidently greater in countries where 'open' proportional systems are in operation, but even FPTP constituencies feature at least four candidates in competition.

Critically, elections give voters an opportunity to 'vote the rascals out'. In this case, FPTP has distinct advantages over rival systems, as the nature of the government is determined by the electorate, not by party elites. Even when FPTP throws up a situation like that experienced in 2010, the resulting government represented over 50% of voters.

The development of modern society has made it impossible for direct democracy to function effectively. For over 100 years, liberal democracies have therefore relied on elections as the next best thing. However, a combination of voter disillusionment with mainstream political parties and the development of more direct forms of communication have meant that the dominance of representative democracy could be under serious threat.

The skills used to participate in elections help citizens develop capacities that are essential for achieving accountable, democratic governance. The process of choosing between candidates or parties requires voters to evaluate respective policies and actions. Voters apply these skills when making a judgement about the performance of ministers and the government as a whole.

Elections are an effective way for democracy to bring about improvements to citizens' lives, as parties and candidates have an electoral incentive to offer, and discuss, policies which aim to improve the quality of life for most voters.

Task 1.1

(In the style of AQA Unit 1: People, Politics and Participation)

Read the extract below and answer the questions which follow.

> A dictatorship is an autocratic political system in which there is no reliable constitutional means to get rid of the dictator. An elective system is one where the electorate is able to choose its representatives regularly. It is not possible to have both these characteristics in one system. An elective dictatorship cannot exist. The term 'elective dictatorship' is empty rhetoric, and Lord Hailsham should stop using it.
>
> Source: adapted from a letter to a national newspaper of 1977

1 Explain the term *elective dictatorship* used in the extract. *(5 marks)*

2 Using the extract and your own knowledge, explain **two** advantages of the type of representative democracy found in the UK. *(10 marks)*

Task 1.2

(In the style of Edexcel Unit 1: People and Politics)

1 To what extent does a participation crisis exist in the UK today? *(25 marks)*

Guidance on how to approach these tasks is provided online at www.hodderplus.co.uk/philipallan.

Further reading

- The Power Report (especially Chapter 1, 'The myth of apathy'): www.powerinquiry.org
- Speaker's Conference (on Parliamentary Representation) Final Report: http://tinyurl.com/33c6vzx

Chapter 2

How democratic is direct democracy?

This chapter explores the extent to which the perceived weaknesses of representative democracy in the UK have been addressed through greater recourse to methods more commonly associated with participatory or direct democracy. While the main focus is on the proliferation of referendums throughout the country, and the benefits or otherwise accrued by their increased use, the chapter also explores the various experiments in increasing participation at a national, regional and local level.

What are the main forms of direct democracy?

Referendums

Referendums ask voters a single question on a specific issue, and usually require a simple yes/no response. An example of this is the question asked in the only national referendum in the UK to date:

> Do you think that the UK should remain in the EEC?

This question was put to the UK electorate in June 1975; of those who voted, 67.2% said 'yes'.

There are several different types of referendum:

- **Indicative referendums** are only used to gauge public opinion on a particular issue.
- **Binding referendums** actually lead to legislative change. These are often held *after* the legislation has been passed by the legislature — the purpose of the referendum is effectively to provide popular ratification.
- Referendums called for by the electorate are commonly referred to as **initiatives**.

Private referendums

Private referendums are used infrequently as a device for raising awareness of public attitudes, primarily because of the cost involved in holding them. In 2000, Scottish businessman Brian Souter demonstrated the effect that a wealthy individual can have on referendum results. As part of his campaign to prevent the Scottish Parliament repealing the controversial Section 2a of the Local Government Act 1988, Mr Souter financed his own private referendum on the issue. Spending approximately £500,000 on the campaign brought him the backing of 87% of those who voted. Turnout, however, was only 34%.

The pressure group I Want A Referendum organised a referendum on the Lisbon Treaty in ten Labour and Liberal Democrat marginal constituencies in February 2008. While the organisers claimed that the poll was a means to give an expression to popular support for a referendum over the surrender of further powers to the EU, Liberal Democrat and Labour opponents dismissed the exercise as a 'political stunt', and MPs in two of the constituencies, East Renfrewshire and Eastleigh, actively encouraged constituents not to participate.

Petitions

The development of the 'e-petition' has helped to increase participation in the political process significantly. From the creation of the Public Petitions system used in Scotland, which allows citizens to ask the Scottish Parliament to look into areas of local and national interest, or legislate where necessary, to the creation of 10 Downing Street's e-petition (http://petitions.number10.gov.uk/), technology has revolutionised the link between the rulers and the ruled.

The 2009 Local Democracy, Economic Development and Construction Act requires councils to make provision for the establishment of local petitions. During the 2010 general election campaign, Alan Johnson, the former home secretary, raised the possibility of petitioning being introduced into the realm of law and order.

The effects of petitions have been mixed. Simply contributing to a petition creates a feel-good factor, when citizens can see that their concerns are being taken seriously. The Scottish model demonstrates how effective e-petitions can be, as increased funding for cancer drugs and the introduction of new taps in schools illustrates. However, the absence of parliamentary involvement (in England) undermines the overall effectiveness of petitions, as it removes much hope that they will result in any kind of legislative action. Some MPs and local councillors also argue that the growth of e-petitions could undermine the workings of representative democracy. The Scottish Parliament experienced an unusual problem in the early stages of e-petitioning, when it was found that one man, Frank Harvey, was responsible for sending 27 of the first 130 petitions under review by the public petitions committee.

Primaries

The Conservative Party introduced its first US-style primary election to select a parliamentary candidate, for the constituency of Reading East, in November 2003. It was open to all eligible voters, who registered as a 'party supporter' in order to participate in the final selection meeting. In 2007, Boris Johnson was chosen as Conservative candidate in a contest open to all Londoners on the electoral roll who had previously registered on a telephone hotline.

Support for primaries has spread across the political spectrum, with Labour MPs Frank Field and David Miliband arguing for their wider use in UK politics. Mr Field believes this will enhance the legitimacy of MPs, the bulk of whom are ultimately elected by a minority of their constituency, and wrest control over candidate selection from party activists.

The first genuinely open primary was held in August 2009 in Totnes. Freepost ballot papers were delivered to all voters in the constituency, who were able to decide which party member from a previously composed shortlist would become the new Conservative candidate.

However, a prominent critic of the primary system, John Strafford, who chairs the Campaign for Conservative Democracy group, described it as a 'nail in the coffin for party membership and party democracy' as, to him, it illustrated Conservative Central Office's unnecessary interference in the constituency association's selection process. He also expressed concern over the cost of the primary, estimated to be around £40,000; Mr Strafford believes there are only 'half a dozen constituencies in the country that (could) possibly afford that kind of money'.

The Conservative–Liberal Democrat coalition announced in May 2010 that the state would pay for postal primaries to held in 200 safe seats.

Initiatives

Most commonly found in the USA and Switzerland, the initiative process allows citizens to amend state constitutions or adopt new laws. Initiatives differ from petitions because they are part of the law-making process, rather than simply requests for inquiries for further information.

Although there is no real history of initiatives' use in the UK, several pressure groups, including Unlock Democracy and Our Say, strongly advocate the introduction of initiatives as a way of connecting citizens with the political process. In 2008, Douglas Carswell MP introduced a private member's bill, the Citizens' Initiative (Legislation) Bill, which would have allowed members of the public to initiate legislation.

The new coalition has picked up on Mr Carswell's plan, and included it in its document *Our Programme for Government*. Although the plan outlined by the coalition does not result in initiatives becoming law immediately, the document states that the most popular initiative with support of at least 100,000 people will be presented as a bill for debate in Parliament.

The citizens' initiative mechanism, created under the terms of the Lisbon Treaty, will also allow UK citizens to submit a legal proposal to the European Commission, assuming they have collected at least a million signatures coming from a 'significant' number of member states.

Electing local officials

One of the most interesting features of the Conservative Party's 2010 manifesto was its commitment to give people greater control over the running of local services. However, the final coalition programme watered down these proposals. Commitment to making the 'police more accountable through oversight by a directly elected individual' has been tempered by the Liberal Democrat policy of increasing local authority control over senior police officials.

People's panels

A few months after coming to power in 1997, the Labour government announced plans to establish a panel of 5,000 citizens to provide regular feedback, over a period of time, on national and local policy, and participate in departmental research projects. This panel was terminated in 2002.

The project was refined in 2006, when Tony Blair created new panels to help advise the government on key areas of its public services reform programme. The 100-strong panels were given access to briefing papers and attended 'summits' with junior ministers and civil servants. Local councils were encouraged to adapt this model of public consultation, with examples such as the 'Derby Pointer Panel' recruiting 1,200 citizens to review provision of services and participate in consultations.

However, concerns have been raised over the poor representation of socially-excluded groups, particularly those for whom English is not the first language, turnover of panel members, especially among the young, and the fact that the agenda is predominantly set by the 'sponsor' rather than the community being consulted.

Consultations

These are a widely used and longstanding form of public participation. Public bodies seek feedback from groups and individuals on a specific issue or range of measures. Building on the experience of the Scottish and Welsh legislatures, the coalition document *Our Programme for Government* announced a new 'public reading stage' on proposed legislation online.

However, critics of consultations claim that they are designed to receive the feedback which the originators want to hear, and are used as means for building public support for proposals. This was a major criticism of the public consultation on a congestion charge for Manchester in 2008.

Public inquiries

Public inquiries are an established, formal type of participation within the UK political system. Usually presided over by a senior judge, they investigate miscarriages of justice, make decisions over major infrastructure developments, such as road-building, or review controversial government decisions.

Their main advantages include transparency of decision making, open access, the independence of the presiding judge, and the close link between the verdict of the inquiry and the eventual government policy.

Box 2.1

The Hutton Inquiry, 2004

Tony Blair established the inquiry to investigate the circumstances surrounding the death of Dr David Kelly, a government scientist at the heart of allegations over the infamous 'sexed-up' dossier justifying war on Iraq.

Retired judge Lord Hutton chaired the inquiry in August–September 2004, during which a large number of government documents, e-mails, and diaries were published online as they were summoned for evidence purposes.

Hutton's final verdict largely absolved the government of any involvement in Dr Kelly's death, instead attributing most of the blame to the BBC. As a result of his findings, the chairman and director-general of the BBC, as well as the government's director of communications, Alastair Campbell, resigned.

However, the presiding judge is appointed by the government, which invariably has a vested interest in the outcome, while the scope of the inquiry is often restricted to very narrow areas. Compared to large institutions, such as a government department, individual campaigners have limited resources to research and prepare their case.

Focus groups

Focus groups allow political parties and government agencies to gauge public attitudes, beliefs and behaviour towards existing or prospective policies. They are used by all layers of government, and in the devolved assemblies. Their main advantages include the high level of interactivity given the small size of the group, and the fact that the membership of the group can be chosen according to the range of opinion required. However, the discussions may be dominated by a small, vocal minority of participants, and there is always the risk that they present a skewed picture of public opinion, given the nature of their construction and composition.

Citizens' juries

Citizens' juries were at the heart of the Labour government's attempts to broaden participation in politics. They consisted of 12–20 members of the public, selected to represent different elements of the community and hear evidence from experts in a particular field. One of the most prominent examples from the Blair era was the jury established by the Food Standards Agency to hear evidence about genetically modified (GM) food. This resulted in the publication of the *People's Report on GM Crops*, a document produced at Newcastle University. After becoming prime minister in 2007, Gordon Brown broadened the range of issues researched by citizen's juries, announcing plans for consultations on crime and immigration, education, health and transport.

Brown defended the use of juries on the grounds that access to the opinions of ordinary citizens would increase popular engagement with the political process, while helping the government become responsive and more aware of people's concerns.

Conservatives argue that citizens' juries offer only superficial participation in the political process, as the recommendations from the juries are not binding on departments, and therefore do not really empower citizens. The Liberal Democrats broadly support the idea, but would like to see the juries become institutionalised, with permanent membership, and shadowing particular departments for a fixed period of time.

Why do governments hold referendums?

Governments hold referendums for several reasons.

To legitimise constitutional changes

The referendum has become the principal device through which approval is sought for reforms to the UK's constitution. Examples which have taken place since 1997 include:

- 1997 Scottish and Welsh devolution
- 1998 Mayor for London; Good Friday Agreement
- 2004 North East regional assembly
- 1999–2010 local elected mayors

To entrench constitutional changes

There are obviously links here to the previous reason. Not only can governments claim a legitimate right to amend the constitution if the matter has been put to a popular vote, but they can effectively entrench this reform in the same way. For example, the only way to reverse devolution in Scotland and Wales is through a further referendum — a stipulation that would prevent a hostile government in England from abolishing either legislature, and that arguably fire-proofed the Scottish Parliament and Welsh Assembly during their difficult first few years.

To settle complex ethical and moral issues

Referendums can be a useful political tool for governments in countries with a strong religious tradition. Where a tension exists between reformist secular groups and a religious organisation, the referendum can offer a means of settling controversial social issues. Although this is not a common motive for holding referendums in the UK, in 2000 wealthy Scottish businessman Brian Souter sponsored a private referendum in Scotland on the Scottish Parliament's plans to repeal Section 28 of the Local Government Act, 1988, which forbade local authorities to 'intentionally promote homosexuality'.

To overcome political disunity

UK party politics is characterised by its adversarial nature and the requirement to maintain an impression of party unity. Occasionally, an issue comes along which threatens to divide a ruling party and could destabilise an otherwise secure administration. In this context, the referendum can provide a means of tolerating significant internal dissent, while allowing opposing groups to make their case to the country.

The referendum on changing the method of electing MPs, to be held in May 2011, is a good example of a popular vote being used to prevent a key element of the Liberal Democrat manifesto dividing the coalition government.

Why have referendums been used more regularly since 1997?

Historically, the referendum has not been a regular method of making policy in the UK. However, since the election of New Labour in 1997, the referendum has become a much more regularly used political device, with five regional and almost 40 local referendums having taken place since then.

Good Friday Agreement referendum — Seamus Mallon and John Hume of the Social Democratic and Labour Party on 23 May 1998

The proliferation of referendums since 1997 can be explained by a wide range of factors.

First, the Labour government inherited one very specific and delicate problem from the outgoing Conservative administration: the peace process in Northern Ireland. The Good Friday Agreement, signed in April 1998, was a compromise package that ended the first stage of the peace process. Faced with two distinct political communities that shared a history of intractable hostility, the May referendum proved to be a unique political experience in the province, with both unionist and nationalist/

republican communities providing majority support for the establishment of a new devolved system of government. The position of the UK government, over the course of many administrations, was that the principle of popular consent would govern any changes to the relationship between Northern Ireland and the mainland. The referendum provided that consent, and tied both sides in the conflict to the terms of the agreement.

Second, many of the issues central to Labour's agenda since 1997 involved a redistribution of power within the UK. One of Labour's 'big ideas' when it came to power was a radical overhaul of the constitution. Labour could certainly have relied on its huge parliamentary majorities to implement this, and indeed did so with the 1998 Human Rights Act, which incorporated the European Convention on Human Rights into UK law. However, in spite of the motives behind them, the 1975 and 1979 referendums had established a precedent that issues of this nature ought to be put before the public.

Third, the apparent success of devolution has required further use of referendums to legitimise the extension of powers to the regional assemblies. Exploiting a clause in the 2006 Government of Wales Act, the Welsh Assembly voted unanimously in February 2010, for a referendum on full lawmaking powers. This is planned to take place by May 2011 at the latest. In Scotland, the ruling Scottish National Party published a referendum bill in September 2010, which sought to gain approval for independence from the UK. However, the referendum is unlikely to be held before the next Scottish Parliament elections.

Finally, short-term political considerations also played their part. Prior to the 1997 general election, the Labour leadership was concerned about the party's vulnerability on two key issues:

- Where future UK membership of the euro was concerned, the party was under threat from a Conservative Party that had already pledged itself to a referendum on the issue, and from Sir James Goldsmith's Referendum Party, which promised to put Britain's membership of the EU to a nationwide vote. Anxious not to appear more euro-friendly and less democratic than either of the two other parties, the then chancellor of the exchequer, Gordon Brown, committed Labour to securing popular consent before abandoning the pound.
- The second issue revolved around the possibility of a future devolved Scottish Parliament possessing tax-raising powers. This controversial proposal threatened to undermine the party's image as a fiscally prudent, economically sound alternative to the Conservatives. By referring final

judgement to the Scottish electorate, Blair and Brown managed to defuse a potentially damaging political issue.

Fears for their respective political futures prompted both Labour and the Conservatives to promise a referendum on the electoral system in 2010. In the months leading up to the 2010 general election, Gordon Brown announced plans to hold a referendum on the possible use of the alternative vote (AV) system (which he later promised to introduce *without* a referendum as part of negotiations with the Liberal Democrats after the election). In a dramatic reversal of the Conservatives' traditional hostility to any reform of the voting system, William Hague publicly announced that a referendum on the replacement of FPTP by AV was offered to the Liberal Democrats during negotiations on a possible post-election deal.

Assessing the value of referendums

What are the advantages of referendums?

They increase popular participation in decision making

Greater use of referendums has allowed citizens to contribute actively to decisions not just on how they are governed, but also on important issues such as how much tax they should pay. Croydon council held a landmark vote in 2001 when it asked 17,000 council tenants, the largest such poll, to vote on a rent freeze and on levels of council tax. Voters in Edinburgh (2005) and Manchester (2008) were given the opportunity to determine the transport priorities in their cities in referendums over possible congestion charges.

They overcome flaws in the mandate theory

One of the major flaws in mandate theory is that it assumes voters agree with all the policies of the party they vote for. As is demonstrated in Chapter 5, voters tend to base their electoral preferences more on generalised images than on a detailed scrutiny of the different manifestos. Inevitably, this could be argued to undermine the mandate model, as the electorate has not genuinely approved specific party policies. By holding regular referendums, representative democracies would be able to overcome this problem, and in the process provide greater legitimacy for the government's actions.

Speaking in support of his Private Member's Bill, Douglas Carswell neatly summarised this view (HC Deb 30 April 2008 c309):

My Bill would give this institution a little backbone. We would still be, in Edmund Burke's memorable phrase, a 'deliberative assembly'; it is just that those assembled here would deliberate what counted with the country.

They provide a definitive answer to a politically sensitive or complex issue

Parties may feel that certain issues are too delicate to be left to MPs, who may feel compelled to vote along party lines, or will feel able to overturn the legislation in future parliaments. In other cases, ethnic or religious influences might determine the direction of their vote.

Perhaps the best demonstration of this advantage of referendums in recent UK political history was the referendum on the Good Friday Agreement in May 1998. This was consistent with the UK government's policy of consent and ensured that all sections of the community were tied into the peace process. Stipulating that a majority of unionists and a majority of nationalists had to vote 'yes', the government was able to provide a definitive, binding answer to the question of Northern Ireland's future political direction.

They serve a valuable citizenship function by educating voters about political issues

A by-product of referendum campaigns is increased political awareness. Saturated with literature and news coverage, voters cannot help but take notice of the main arguments surrounding an issue. This can have important social consequences too. In October 2005, the Brazilian government held a vote on the continued sale of firearms in the country. Although the result was in favour of the continued sale of firearms, it was felt that the referendum formed a useful part of the government's 'Project Disarmament' against high levels of violence in Brazil.

They can prevent parties from dividing over a single issue

While critics of referendums might present this as an undesirable use of referendums, one can make the point that repeated splintering of political parties might bring with it equally undesirable political instability.

The wooing of the Liberal Democrats after the 2010 general election illustrated this argument perfectly. The Conservatives, traditionally hostile to electoral reform, offered the Liberal Democrats a referendum on the use of the alternative vote (AV) for Westminster elections, while Labour, prepared to recognise some flaws in FPTP but sceptical about PR, said no referendum would be required for the introduction of AV, but one would be required for the replacement of FPTP by a proportional system of voting.

Cameron's decision to allow a vote on AV served two purposes: it was a concession to his coalition partners, while at the same time allowing his party to campaign against AV in the ensuing referendum.

What are the disadvantages of referendums?

They undermine the principle of parliamentary sovereignty

The principle of parliamentary sovereignty could be affected in two ways. First, the ultimate responsibility for making legislation would pass to the electorate. Second, the right of parliament to repeal previous legislation would also be undermined, as a post-legislation referendum could lead to the legislation being removed from the statute book, as happened with the 1978 Scotland Act, after the then government lost the 1979 referendum.

The result can be influenced by the wording of the question

Asking whether voters wish to see an increase in their council taxes, or whether they want to see schools and hospitals close could make an enormous difference to how people vote. Although the Electoral Commission has the power to pass comment on the wording of questions, it lacks the power to make its recommendations binding on the government.

During the North East regional assembly referendum, the director of the 'no' campaign had this to say about the monitoring of the campaign:

> The problems with the Electoral Commission are too numerous to go into… nobody should be under any illusion that the commission exists to police conduct at referenda. When we complained (about government interference in the campaign), it said there was nothing it could do.

Critics of the SNP's plans for a referendum on independence have questioned the decision of the Scottish Executive to create a new Scottish Referendum Commission to oversee the referendum rather than the Electoral Commission, which would normally monitor Scottish Parliament elections. One possible explanation for the move was provided as a result of a freedom of information request which indicated that the Electoral Commission had concerns over the wording of the referendum questions.

Democratic motives do not always influence the decision to call a referendum

The 2001 referendum in Bristol was prompted by the ruling Labour group, which was reluctant to lose control of the council by having to make a choice between raising council taxes and risking alienating voters, and keeping taxes static and having to trim public services — something likely to lead to a split in the local Labour party.

Low turnouts undermine the legitimacy of the result and can lead to a 'tyranny of the minority'

Turnout for the 1998 referendum on a Mayor for London was 34.1%, with the figure falling to around 25% in some parts of Greater London. The 'yes' campaign achieved an overwhelming majority of the vote (72%), but the decision to change the way London was governed was approved by only 24% of registered voters. While many countries insist on a minimum turnout threshold, this has never been the case in any of the referendums held in mainland Britain since 1997. Before the vote on a regional assembly for the North East, the government said that it would not accept a result that had a derisory turnout. However, it did not specify what it meant by 'derisory'.

Inequalities in funding can unduly influence the final result

Evidence from the 1997 Welsh devolution campaign and various referendums on European integration point to the significant impact that a clear financial advantage can have on the result. In Ireland, the successful government-backed 'yes' campaign for the second vote on ratifying the Nice Treaty outspent the 'no' campaign by a ratio of 20:1. Although the Electoral Commission has laid down strict rules regarding the funding and expenditure levels of future referendum campaigns, the government could still use public money to make its case before the official start of the campaign (even though this would conflict with the 1998 Neill Report recommendation that the government should remain neutral).

Conclusion: has the increased use of direct democratic devices in the UK since 1997 enhanced democracy?

The chapter began by suggesting that the increased use of participatory approaches was, if only in part, driven by a need to plug the gaps in the version of democracy used in the UK. To a certain extent, the increased use of direct democratic devices has achieved this aim. Since participation in conventional party politics is in serious decline, alternative approaches have had to be found to engage the electorate in decision making. Opening up the range of issues upon which people can decide directly and widening the mechanisms of participation illustrate the flexibility of the UK state to respond to democratic challenges.

It is significant that more attention is being paid to the process by which major constitutional decisions are taken. While the majority of Scottish, Welsh, Northern Irish, and London voters clearly wanted devolved powers, the way that those powers were given to them, through a plebiscite, virtually guarantees that these powers will remain entrenched unless the consent of the majority is given to remove them.

In spite of these undoubted benefits of utilising more consultative approaches to decision making, perhaps we should not be too impressed by their claims to enhance genuine participation in the political process. The use of referendums in the UK has largely been for tactical, rather than democratic purposes, and concerns over their funding, timing, criteria for success, and wording have further undermined their democratic credentials. The issue of low turnout applies to referendums and the other forms of participatory democracy trialled to a much greater degree than to general, and most other, elections.

Ultimately, the opportunities provided by the new forms of direct democracy in the UK allow people to take greater responsibility for decisions that affect their everyday lives. In this sense, they have certainly enhanced democracy in the UK. However, the experience of these new initiatives suggests that people are not too concerned about acquiring this added responsibility, and remain sceptical of any attempts by the established parties to rebuild confidence in the UK's political system.

Task 2.1

(In the style of Edexcel Unit 1: People and Politics)

1   Giving an example, provide a definition of primaries.   *(5 marks)*
2   Explain the methods used to increase participation in the UK political
    system.   *(10 marks)*

Task 2.2

(In the style of OCR Unit F851: Contemporary Politics of the UK, Section B)

1   Discuss the advantages and disadvantages of making greater use
    of referendums in the UK.   *(30 marks)*

Guidance on how to approach these tasks is provided online at
www.hodderplus.co.uk/philipallan.

Useful websites

- Campaign for direct democracy in Britain:
  www.iniref.org
- People and Participation.net:
  www.peopleandparticipation.net

Is first-past-the-post defensible?

According to supporters of FTFP, one of the system's virtues is the fact that it has proved durable and effective over a long period. However, the erosion of the two-party system, for so long synonymous with the preservation of FPTP, and the introduction of varied systems for the new regional assemblies throughout the UK have focused greater attention on the arguments for reforming the system used to elect MPs. The experience of the 2010 general election has arguably moved the argument to a tipping point — the prospect of future elections being held under FPTP is increasingly uncertain.

MPs gather in the House of Commons for the first time after the 2010 general election

What are the main problems with FPTP?

The principal arguments in favour of electoral reform are as follows:

- The party that wins a majority of the seats in Parliament rarely wins an overall majority of votes cast. As a result, one could claim that the governing party lacks a popular mandate to govern:
  - 1997 Labour 43.2%
  - 2001 Labour 40.7%
  - 2005 Labour 35.3%
- The percentage vote that a party receives is not accurately reflected in its percentage share of the seats in the House of Commons. For example, 35% of the electorate voted for Labour in 2005, yet that party received 55% of the seats. This is a deviation from proportionality (DV) of +20. Labour actually received fewer votes than in 1979 — an election that the party lost.
- By way of contrast, smaller parties tend to lose out under FPTP. In 2005, the Liberal Democrats only gained 9% of the seats even after gaining 22% of the votes —a DV of –13. In 2010, the Liberal Democrat share of the vote increased 1% from 2005, yet the party won five fewer seats (see Table 3.1).

Table 3.1 Relationship between votes and seats, 2010 general election

	% votes	% seats	DV
Conservatives	36.1	47.3	+11.2
Labour	29.0	39.8	+10.8
Liberal Democrats	23.0	8.8	−14.2

- The electoral system appears to be biased in favour of Labour. Historically, both main parties have benefited more or less equally from the distorting effect of FPTP, but since 1997 it has clearly worked to Labour's advantage (see Box 3.1). In 2005, there was only 2.9% difference in their share of the popular vote, yet Labour enjoyed a massive 25% advantage in the number of seats won. In 2010, Labour needed almost 2,000 fewer votes to win a seat than the Conservatives, and a massive 90,000 fewer votes than the Liberal Democrats. In effect, this means that everyone's votes are not equal — a major flaw in the exercise of representative democracy in the UK.
- The system tends to favour large parties that enjoy support which is evenly spread throughout the country. One factor that contributed to Labour's electoral dominance between 1997 and 2010 was the party's ability to win seats throughout the UK. By contrast, Scotland and Wales have been virtual electoral deserts for the Conservative Party, while the Liberal Democrats have found it traditionally difficult to win seats in Wales, the South East and the North East (see Table 3.2).

Box 3.1

Factors that swing the electoral system Labour's way

- Labour-held seats tend to have fewer constituents than Conservative-held seats.
- Voters are increasingly prepared to vote tactically and negatively to keep their most disliked party out. Historically, this has hit the Conservatives hardest, with Labour voters switching to the Liberal Democrats either to unseat Conservatives or to keep them out.
- Decline in the turnout has occurred mostly among Labour supporters, thus depriving Labour of votes, but not being sufficiently large to cost it seats. The Conservatives, on the other hand, tend to win seats in areas with higher turnouts.
- Prior to the 2005 election, both Scotland and Wales, regions where Labour does very well, were over-represented at Westminster. Recent changes to constituency boundaries removed Scotland's over-representation, but left Wales with approximately 8 seats too many.
- Research by Ron Johnston, Iain McLean, Charles Pattie and David Rossiter for an article in *Political Quarterly* (Volume 80, Issue 4, November 2009) suggests that Labour's ability to win seats with fairly slender majorities, and to generally distribute its vote evenly throughout the country, gives it an inbuilt advantage in spite of the recent boundary changes.

Table 3.2 Geographical reach of the major parties, 2010 (seats won)

	Scotland	Wales	South East	North East
Conservatives	1	8	75	2
Labour	41	26	4	25
Liberal Democrats	11	3	4	2

- FPTP tends to support a two-party system. No other party has held office apart from Labour and Conservative since 1929, while at least 70% of the population has voted for the two main parties since the Second World War. In the 2005 election, 80% of the seats were won by Labour and Conservative candidates, while in 2010 the two main parties gained 65% of the vote, yet won 87% of the seats.
- On occasions, FPTP fails in one of its primary purposes: to produce a government formed by the party receiving a plurality of votes. In 1951 and February 1974, the party with the second highest number of votes actually won the most seats and formed the government (see Table 3.3).

Election	Country	% votes	% seats
1951	UK	Labour 48.8	47.20
		Conservative 48	51.36
1974 (Feb)	UK	Labour 37.2	47.40
		Conservative 37.8	46.77
1981	New Zealand	National Party 47	38.80
		Labour 43	39.00

Table 3.3 Winner takes all? Occasions when the party with a plurality of votes did not win the most seats

- The experience of the 2010 election suggests that FPTP may no longer be able to deliver on its two strongest claims: to enable voters to remove unpopular governments and to produce strong, stable governments. Even though Labour's share of the vote fell by 6% between 2005 and 2010, there was still a realistic chance of Gordon Brown forming a government, either in a minority with the Liberal Democrats, or as part of a 'rainbow coalition' alongside the various nationalist parties of the UK. After 6 May, five possible scenarios emerged for the shape of the new government, none of which looked likely to provide the type of government supporters of FPTP claim it is especially well equipped to deliver:
  - Scenario 1: Conservatives rule alone as a minority government.
  - Scenario 2: Conservatives rule alone, with a 'confidence and supply' basis.
  - Scenario 3: Conservatives rule in a coalition with the Liberal Democrats.
  - Scenario 4: Labour creates a minority government with Liberal Democrats.
  - Scenario 5: Labour, Liberal Democrats, SNP, Plaid Cymru, SDLP and Greens form a 'rainbow coalition'.
- A major criticism of FPTP is that most of the votes cast do not actually count. These 'wasted' votes result from the fact that the winning candidate in a constituency does not require 50% of the vote. This means that in most constituencies, the votes of most voters do not contribute to the result. The other group of voters whose preference is irrelevant consists of those voters who voted for the winning candidate *after* the candidate had already acquired sufficient support to win the seat. The extent of this problem is illustrated by the statistics from the 2005 and 2010 general elections:
  - 2005: 70% of votes cast were 'wasted'
  - 2010: 71% of votes cast were 'wasted'

Some losing candidates in 2010 could count themselves particularly unlucky, as they managed to receive more votes than winning candidates in other constituencies. Annunziata Rees-Mogg in Somerton and Frome narrowly lost after acquiring 26,976 votes. By way of contrast, Glenda Jackson MP, who won the Hampstead and East Kilburn seat, received 17,332 votes (32.8%) in a tight three-way marginal contest. The issue of wasted votes further adds to the problems faced by smaller parties as they appear to be the chief victims. Of all those votes wasted, those cast for the Liberal Democrats comprised 36% of the total. The British National Party received 565,376 votes nationally, yet won no seats and was the hardest hit of the minor parties.

● FPTP creates a large number of safe seats, seats which are unlikely to change hands during an election. In 2010 only 18% of seats contested actually changed hands, with no seats at all changing hands in Scotland, apart from Glasgow North East, previously held by the former Speaker of the House of Commons, Michael Martin, which was won by Labour in 2010.

● The principal issue with safe seats is that they tend to produce a lower turnout among voters, as electors have little incentive to turn out to vote. As Table 3.4 illustrates, safe seats tend to be in urban areas, with higher-than-average levels of social deprivation. In the opinion of Dr Stuart Wilks-Heeg from the London School of Economics: 'That political inequality and socio-economic inequality have become so closely interwoven is yet another damning indictment of our electoral system' ('What about the voters?' http://blogs.lse.ac.uk/politicsandpolicy/?tag=safe-seats).

| Table 3.4 | Location of the safest seats in the UK |

Seat (in descending order of security)	Party that won the seat	Majority (%)	Turnout (NB highest turnout 77.3%; lowest turnout 46%; UK average 65.1%)
Liverpool, Walton	Labour	57.7	54.8
Knowsley (Merseyside)	Labour	57.5	56.1
East Ham (London)	Labour	55.2	55.6
Belfast West	Sinn Fein	54.7	54.0
Glasgow North East	Labour	54.2	49.1
Liverpool, West Derby	Labour	51.6	56.7
Orkney and Shetland	Liberal Democrat	51.3	58.5
Bootle (near Liverpool)	Labour	51.3	57.8
Kirkcaldy and Cowdenbeath (Gordon Brown's seat)	Labour	50.2	62.2
Coatbridge, Chryston and Bellshill	Labour	49.8	59.4

- There is strong evidence that FPTP fails to provide a reasonable representation of British society in the House of Commons. Although the link between social representation and the electoral system could be argued to be tenuous, there is a significant difference in the range of representatives elected to assemblies throughout the UK where proportional systems are deployed, and the Westminster Parliament, where a plurality system is used (see Table 3.5).

Table 3.5	Representation of women and ethnic minorities under different electoral systems in the UK		
Election	**System**	**% women elected**	**% ethnic-minority group members elected**
General election, 2010	FPTP	21.9	4.0
Scottish Parliament, 2007	AMS	33.3	0.78
Welsh Assembly, 2007	AMS	46.7	1.67
London Assembly, 2008	STV	37	8.0
European Parliament, 2009	Closed list	26	4.6

- One of the factors that impacts on the extent of diversity among representatives is the element of voter choice in selecting particular candidates. Where there is a greater element of voter choice, with single transferable vote (STV) or additional member system (AMS) for example, a more diverse range of candidate is elected. It is easier for a party to select a balanced ticket of candidates if it has the opportunity to contest multi-member constituencies, rather than a single seat constituency where there might be a temptation to select a candidate similar to the incumbent MP (e.g. white, male, middle-class).

Why should we keep FTFP?

Despite its disadvantages, several arguments can be made in favour of FTFP:

- It is easy to understand and operate. A single 'X' by the name of the preferred candidate is sufficient to indicate your choice. The number of crosses is added up and the result is obtained — usually within a few hours of the polling stations closing. Sunderland South is traditionally the first constituency to declare its result, doing so at 10.51 p.m. on 6 May 2010. Even if the formation of the new government is not always apparent, the overwhelming number of constituencies have declared their individual results by the time the electorate wakes up the morning after the election.

- FPTP generally secures strong and stable government. Each of the governments elected since October 1974 has been able to last at least 4 years without the need for a further general election. All but two of those governments have also enjoyed a very comfortable majority in the House of Commons. This has made it easier for them to carry out their manifesto promises. Although David Cameron's Conservative Party failed to achieve an overall majority in 2010, the coalition with the Liberal Democrats created a parliamentary majority of 78, suggesting that once again the electoral system will create a stable administration, albeit not in the manner which supporters of FPTP may have envisaged.

- During the 2010 election campaign, David Cameron returned to a common theme when defending the continued suitability of FPTP: it makes it relatively easy to get rid of unpopular governments. As the elections of 1979 and 1997 ably demonstrate, the two-party system enables voters to switch allegiances if they want to replace the governing party with an alternative.

- Defenders of the system point to the strong links that exist between an MP and his or her constituency. First, voters know the identity of each candidate and in most cases have contributed to the selection process. Constituents can therefore contact their MP directly should they wish to raise a particular issue. Most importantly, they can hold their own MP to account for his or her record in parliament at the next general election, and, if necessary, vote him or her out. Second, the MP–constituency link is preserved by FPTP through the comparatively small size of constituencies. Whereas single-member constituencies are a central feature of FPTP, systems such as STV usually consist of between three and five representatives and the 12 electoral regions for the 2009 European Parliament Elections in the UK elected between three and ten MEPs.

- While the result does not provide a statistical representation of the popular will, FPTP has an unerring knack of reflecting the public mood. The huge majority obtained by Labour in 1997 appeared to be a product of both popular disillusionment with the Conservative government and a wave of support for Tony Blair's Labour Party, while the 2010 result appeared to accurately reflect a mood which wanted to punish Labour but was not wholly convinced by the alternatives.

- Ironically, the consequences of the hung parliament illustrated some of the problems that would be more common should the UK switch to a more proportional system for electing MPs. On the one hand, it created a period of uncertainty when the UK was effectively without an elected government between 6 and 11 May 2010. The failure of any party to achieve an overall majority also resulted in the type of 'backroom deals' and 'horse-trading' described by David Cameron in such negative terms in several pre-election speeches. Ultimately, however, it is the disproportionate influence exercised by the Liberal Democrats, whose parliamentary representation actually fell in 2010, which might illustrate the most unpalatable effects of hung parliaments, and proportional representation by implication. In a situation where they were over 200 seats behind the second-placed party, the Liberal Democrats were effectively able to decide the formation of the next government, even if that had resulted in the formation of a minority government with a party which had lost 91 seats and was 59 seats behind the most popular party.

The first cabinet meeting of the Conservative–Liberal Democrat coalition government after the 2010 general election

Do the parties support reform of the electoral system?

Labour Party

Historically, the Labour Party has been sceptical about the issue of electoral reform. Believing that FPTP worked to its advantage, the party paid little attention to it until its fourth successive general election defeat in 1992. After this, the party leadership commissioned Lord Plant to investigate alternatives to

FPTP for general elections and the elections that would accompany the party's proposed constitutional changes (see Box 3.2). Although his recommendations were not wholly adopted by the party leadership, his commission did provide an ideological impetus to the campaign for reform among Labour Party members.

Box 3.2

Plant Report

The recommendations of the Plant Commission included:
- general elections: supplementary vote (SV)
- European Parliament: regional list
- House of Lords: regional list

Since Plant's report, the party's relationship with electoral reform has been turbulent, to say the least (see Table 3.6). Not only did the introduction of more proportional systems deprive the party of seats in a series of regional and European elections, but Labour's failure to fully implement manifesto commitments over reform of the system used to elect MPs has led many commentators to doubt the sincerity of the party's commitment to genuine electoral reform.

Table 3.6 How committed has Labour been to electoral reform?

Commitment to electoral reform	Date	Questionable commitment to electoral reform
Plant Report recommends scrapping FPTP for Westminster and introducing proportional systems for proposed devolved assemblies	1992	
General election manifesto contains a commitment to create an independent commission on voting reform and hold a referendum on reforming the system	1997	
The Jenkins Commission reports and recommends replacing FPTP with the 'alternative vote plus' (AV+) (see Box 3.3)	1998	– Home secretary Jack Straw and other prominent cabinet ministers critical of AV+ – Straw introduces closed-list PR for European Parliament elections, which maintains party control over candidate selection, rather than alternatives which increase voter choice

– Closed-list PR used to elect UK MEPS for the first time – AMS used to elect members of Scottish Parliament and Welsh Assembly – STV used to elect members of Northern Ireland Assembly	1999	
Supplementary vote used for the first time to elect the Mayor of London	2000	
	2001	– No referendum on AV+ – Dropped commitment to hold a referendum on AV+, instead promising a review of the UK's experience of electoral reform
	2005	– No referendum or review – Repeat commitment to review experience of electoral reform since 1997
Review of UK's experience of electoral reform published	2008	
During the Labour Party conference, Gordon Brown announces that the party is committed to replacing FPTP with the alternative vote	2009	
– Brown amends the Constitutional Reform and Governance Bill to include a plan for a referendum on the introduction of AV – During post-election coalition talks, Brown promises the Liberal Democrats that he would introduce AV with a simple vote in parliament, and then hold a referendum on more proportional alternatives	2010	The amendment is dropped in the 'wash-up' period prior to the dissolution of parliament

Box 3.3

What is AV+?

The multi-party commission, under the chairmanship of Lord Jenkins, recommended replacing FPTP with a completely original electoral system. Influenced by the popularity of mixed systems among countries adopting new electoral systems — such as New Zealand, Japan, Russia, and Hungary — the commission created a variant of the additional member system (AMS) called alternative vote plus (AV+).

Box 3.3 (continued)

In order to achieve fairer representation and a more proportional result, between 15 and 20% of MPs would be elected by list PR. These would be the top-up representatives from the regions. However, stable government, with a strong MP–constituency link, would be maintained by the majority of MPs being elected from single-member constituencies using the alternative vote. Figure 3.1 shows how the use of AV+ would have changed the result of the 2010 general election.

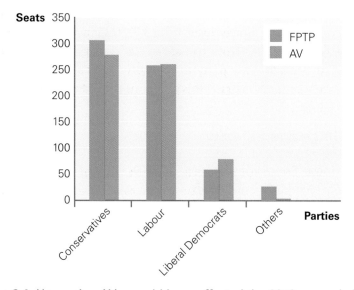

Figure 3.1 How using AV+ would have affected the 2010 general election

Although the leadership of the party was prepared to support moves to replace FPTP with AV in 2010, the party is by no means united over the issue of electoral reform. The breakdown of opinions on the issue can be loosely described as follows:

- Proportionalists — the most prominent advocate of PR within the Labour Party is the Labour Campaign for Electoral Reform. It supports the introduction of AV as a short-term measure, but wants to see a proportional system of voting introduced beyond that.
- Partialists — this group has emerged since about 2000 and sees a limited form of electoral reform as one of a series of measures necessary to restore trust in British politics. The new Labour leader, Ed Miliband, could be included in this group. In an interview with the *Independent* in September 2009 he commented that he prefers a switch to AV, as it is a system 'under

which MPs will be more accountable' ('I'm sympathetic to demands for electoral reform, says Miliband', 29 September 2009).

- Tacticians — this group sees some merits in majoritarian systems, such as AV, as they will maintain the MP–constituency link, and (theoretical models suggest) will elect a greater number of anti-Conservative MPs than any other system, including FPTP. Given Gordon Brown's previous reluctance to speak on the issue, and the late timing of his conversion to the cause of AV, he is a likely member of this group.
- Opposers — this group, once dominant but now declining in number, strongly opposes any move away from FPTP. Opposers believe that the system is more likely to work to Labour's advantage than alternatives, as it would usually allow the party to govern without relying on a coalition partner. Prominent members of this group include Ed Balls and former chief whip Nick Brown.

Conservative Party

Given Tory hostility to most aspects of constitutional reform, it should be no surprise to discover that most Conservatives oppose any move away from FPTP. Like Labour, they believe that FPTP works in their favour, with periods out of office being more than matched by the number of times that the system has secured them power. They also reject reform on the grounds that it leads to weak and unstable coalition governments, which depend heavily on the acquiescence of minor coalition partners.

The Conservatives also strongly support the view of political scientist Michael Pinto-Duschinsky that a prime function of an electoral system is to give the voters the means to remove an ineffective government. Pinto-Duschinsky argues that FPTP performs this role better any other variant:

> One of the great strengths of Britain's tried and tested electoral system, FPTP, is its ability to 'kick the rascals out'... Our political system needs reform, but only the traditional British voting system gives voters the power to force a change of government in a clear and decisive way.
>
> Source: Extract from a letter to *The Times* from Eric Pickles MP, Conservative Party chairman, 27 May 2010

However, several cracks have emerged in this traditional view of Conservative hostility to electoral reform:

- The party has no plans to change the varied systems introduced in the UK since 1997.

- The party is committed to using single transferable vote (STV) to elect members of a new upper House. Ken Clarke, George Young and William Hague all signed up to the cross-party paper 'Reforming the House of Lords: breaking the deadlock' in 2005, and the coalition government has remained faithful to that pledge.

- A small, but growing, number of Conservative MPs support the replacement of FPTP. Organised under the umbrella of the Conservative Action for Electoral Reform group, this group includes Douglas Carswell MP, who co-authored much of Cameron's constitutional reform programme.

- Although David Cameron has strongly expressed his support for FPTP, several of his cabinet colleagues are believed to have shifted their position on AV, arguing that the party had been 'intellectually lazy' to ignore the merits of alternative systems in the past.

- David Cameron was quick to offer a referendum on the introduction of AV to the Liberal Democrats during the negotiations over the creation of a coalition government after 6 May 2010. While this will usher in the first national vote on how we elect our MPs, it is not a clear sign that the prime minister has embraced electoral reform. Instead, Cameron's offer had everything to do with tactics and little to do with 'fair votes'.

Box 3.4

Possible reasons why David Cameron offered a referendum on electoral reform to the Liberal Democrats

Reason 1   Failure to offer any concession on electoral reform would have been a dealbreaker during the coalition talks.

Reason 2   Cameron has retained the right to campaign against AV in any future referendum.

Reason 3   AV could help Cameron create a centre-right block in the House of Commons, reducing his need to rely on his right-wing critics and marginalising Labour.

Reason 4   Cameron might hope that the House of Commons' vote creating the referendum will fail.

Liberal Democrat Party

The Liberal Democrats have had the longest commitment to PR of all the major parties, with a sustained advocacy of the merits of STV since the nineteenth century. In their eyes, it offers greater voter choice and ensures the fairest result. Their position can be explained partially by self-interest — FPTP has done them no favours since the First World War — but their belief in the role of the individual, and limiting the power of elites, also makes STV appear a more attractive proposition.

The 2010 Policy Briefing on Political Reform provided further reasons for supporting STV, as it would give voters a 'choice between people as well as parties, (meaning) they can stick with a party but punish a bad MP by voting for someone else'.

One of the party's key concessions from the Conservatives in May 2010 was obviously the guarantee of a referendum on AV. However, even if the party wins the vote, this would be only the first stage of reform for the Liberal Democrats, particularly as it is not a system which offers to boost the size of the third party in Parliament dramatically, and does not meet the stated objective of increasing voter choice.

Minor parties

All the prominent minor parties support reform of the electoral system. The Greens advocate the introduction of AMS, while at the last election the SNP and Plaid Cymru argued for a more proportional system.

At the other end of the spectrum, UKIP supports the introduction of AV+ for all national and local elections. UKIP has benefited enormously from proportional systems in recent elections, gaining 12 MEPs under closed-list PR in the 2009 European Parliament elections.

The BNP has adopted a highly pragmatic position on the issue. Without explicitly calling for a reform of the electoral system, the party's leader, Nick Griffin, has made clear his view on how much the party could gain from a switch to a different system.

Conclusion: how likely is reform of the electoral system?

On the one hand, the prospect of reform looks highly likely. Opponents of reform used to dismiss the issue as something which the majority of the population had little interest in and even less knowledge about. What most voters were concerned about, they argued, was whether the government which was created after an election was both strong and stable. To an extent this was true, with relatively few people expressing support for the introduction of PR before 1997.

Even after the 2005 general election, most respondents to an NOP poll conducted for the *Independent* in May 2005 expressed support for the view that 'It is right that Labour have an overall majority because they won more votes than anyone else'. The only comforting note for supporters of reform was provided by academics, such as David Farrell and Michael Cunningham, who argued that people's own experience of elections had a direct impact on their attitude to electoral systems. For example, levels of support for the use of AMS tend to be higher in Scotland, where it has been used for elections to the Scottish Parliament, than in England, which has had no such experience.

The experience of 2010, however, radically altered the landscape in which the debate is being fought. A series of polls conducted immediately after the election suggested that public opinion had swung decisively behind electoral reform, while a poll conducted by Politics Home on 9–10 May found that respondents believed it was the fourth most important issue for the party leaders to focus on, ahead of unemployment, tax, health, and law and order.

The conversion of each of the major parties to supporting, at the very least, a referendum on an alternative electoral system also suggests that FPTP's days are numbered. Indeed, growing support for reform from within the Labour Party, and, to a lesser extent the Conservative Party, might indicate that the issue is unlikely to be ignored as easily as it was after the Jenkins Report was published.

However, the promise of the referendum on AV does not guarantee future reform. Cameron and many of his cabinet see continued merits in maintaining FPTP, and he has pledged to campaign against its removal. Should he be successful in the referendum, it may be some time before electoral reform reappears on the political agenda.

On balance, the likelihood of reform may ultimately depend on how well the coalition functions. If voters come to see it as being as stable as a government formed by a single party enjoying an overall majority, and view Parliament as 'balanced' rather than 'hung', then the idea of future coalitions will not be as challenging as it appeared to be in the immediate aftermath of the 2010 general election. If that does become the case, resistance to electoral systems which tend to create 'balanced' parliaments may become less apparent.

Task 3.1

(In the style of OCR Unit F581: Contemporary Politics of the UK, Section A)

Source A: Electoral performance of the BNP under different electoral systems in the UK

Election	Electoral system	BNP % votes	BNP seats
2010 general election	FPTP	1.9	0
2009 European Parliament	PR	6.2	2
2008 Greater London Assembly	AMS	5.3	1

Source B: Liberal Democrats: what we stand for

One party can gain control of Parliament even if only a quarter of the people support them. The electoral system allows Labour and the Tories to take turns at governing. It is not in their interest to change it and as a result, nothing in Britain will change. The worst cases of abuse in the expenses scandal were by MPs in safe seats. Big money has dominated politics for far too long.

Source: **www.libdems.org.uk/political_reform.aspx**

1 Using the sources and your own knowledge, discuss the view that the current system for electing MPs should be retained. *(28 marks)*

Task 3.2

(In the style of Edexcel Unit 1: People and Politics)

1 What are the main features of the first-past-the-post electoral system? *(5 marks)*

2 How does FPTP affect party representation in the House of Commons? *(10 marks)*

Guidance on how to approach these tasks is provided online at **www.hodderplus.co.uk/philipallan**.

Useful websites

- All Party Group on Electoral Reform:
  www.appgelectoralreform.org/resources.html
- The Electoral Reform Society:
  www.electoral-reform.org.uk
- Labour Campaign for Electoral Reform:
  www.electoralreform.org.uk

Do the new UK electoral systems work?

In many respects, critics of FPTP enjoyed something of a free ride before Labour came to power in 1997. Before Labour's creation of new political institutions, and new methods of electing members of those institutions, along with the decision to replace FPTP with closed-list PR for European Parliament elections in the UK, critics had been able to highlight the weaknesses of FPTP without having to defend the practical effects of their own preferred alternative.

From a position in which FPTP was dominant in the UK, a more complicated map of electoral systems has emerged since 1999 (see Table 4.1).

Table 4.1 The diverse electoral map of the UK

System	Where used	Used to elect
Single transferable vote (STV)	Northern Ireland Scotland	Assembly member, local councillors, MEPs Local councillors
Additional member system (AMS)	Scotland Wales London	Members of the Scottish Parliament Assembly members Assembly members
Closed-list PR	Mainland Britain	Members of the European Parliament
Supplementary vote (SV)	London England	Mayor Mayors in 12 towns

This chapter outlines the mechanics of the diverse range of alternatives to FPTP used in the UK since 1997 and evaluates how far they have been a success. Ultimately, it considers whether the experience of electoral reform in the UK has made reform of the system used for electing MPs to Westminster more desirable or not.

Single transferable vote (STV)

The single transferable vote (STV) is currently used for local, assembly and European Parliament elections in Northern Ireland, and for local elections in Scotland.

How does STV work?

STV is probably the most complicated of all the alternatives to FPTP used in the UK at present. Under STV, the region is divided up into large multi-member constituencies, and each constituency elects between three and five representatives depending on its size. Voters can rank the candidates, putting a '1' for their favourite, a '2' for the next, and so on. They can also vote for just one candidate or accept the rank order of their preferred party.

In order to get elected, a candidate needs to receive a certain quota of votes. This quota (Q) is based on the formula:

$$Q = \frac{\text{(number of votes cast)}}{\text{(number of seats in the constituency} + 1)} + 1$$

Once a candidate has gained the quota, any 'surplus' votes are transferred to the second-placed candidate and so on. This process is repeated each time someone gains sufficient votes to be elected. If a candidate receives insufficient first-preference votes and is eliminated, then all of the votes for that candidate are redistributed to the second-placed candidate on the ballot paper.

What have been the main effects of using STV in the UK?

- One of the main strengths of STV is that few votes are wasted, as most of the votes ultimately help to elect a candidate. Depending on the variant of STV used, the underlying principle is that surplus votes from either a candidate reaching the quota, or rejected at the bottom, are transferred to other candidates.
- In common with most forms of PR, STV usually leads to greater diversity among elected representatives. As this system allows voters to place candidates in rank order, for example, they can express a clear preference for a woman candidate should they want to see more women in the legislature. Equally, they could use the rank order to increase the likelihood of minority parties gaining representation. However, the fall in the number of women councillors in Scotland 2003–07 suggests that, by itself, using a proportional electoral system is no guarantee of providing fair representation. While the 2007 elections demonstrated that ultimate control over candidate selection remains firmly in the hands of a party's leadership, who may feel that a white man is more likely to win a seat, particularly if he is the incumbent, it did

suggest that when women make it to the ballot paper, they are more likely to get elected when STV is used than under FPTP (see Table 4.2).

| Table 4.2 | Proportion of women candidates and councillors in Scotland, 2003–07 |

	% women candidates	**% women elected**
2003	27.7	21.8
2007	22.5	21.6

Source: Electoral Reform Society, *Local Authority Elections in Scotland* (2007)

- The introduction of STV to Scotland had a significant impact on voter choice. In the first instance, the average number of candidates in each ward increased from 3.4 in 2003, to 7.4 in 2007. In addition, whereas 61 wards were uncontested in 2003, no wards were uncontested in 2007. Voter choice was also enhanced by the fact that all of the 'big four' parties in Scotland were able to contest virtually every seat across Scotland.
- Recent experience of using STV in the UK suggests that it has a positive effect on turnout. The 2007 Scottish local elections saw a 9.5% increase on the 2003 elections, held under FPTP.
- It can result in a different kind of politics being practised, leading to closer cooperation between parties. During the 1998 Northern Ireland Assembly elections, the SDLP encouraged its supporters to deploy their second-preference votes in favour of parties that supported the Good Friday Agreement.
- Although the practice of recommending that preference votes go to rival parties has not manifested itself yet in Scotland, the introduction of STV has led to increased scrutiny of the ruling executive by councillors, and to a greater need for council leaders to negotiate compromises with council chambers than would be the case after a FPTP election.
- While the voting is reasonably straightforward, the counting process is complicated and can take a long time. This is one of the reasons why STV can only be found in countries with relatively small populations, such as Australia (elections for the Senate), Malta, and the Republic of Ireland.
- Campaigning in much larger constituencies can pose logistical and financial problems for candidates. This was identified as the most significant problem presented by the move to STV by Scottish councillors after the May 2007 elections.
- The need to secure a high ranking can lead to infighting between candidates from the same party, although the evidence from Scotland in 2007 was that this was not a feature of the election campaign. Indeed, feedback from

Scottish councillors outlined in 'The Scottish Councillor Study: feedback after electoral reform' (2007) after the election suggested that parties' candidates were keen to present a collegiate front to the electorate. Whether this remains the case in future, as candidates gain a better understanding of the electoral system's effects, remains to be seen.

- The removal of the close link between councillor and constituent in Scotland has led, in some cases, to councillors free-riding on the back of their fellow councillors' achievements.

- The use of STV in Northern Ireland has arguably impeded the emergence of a more moderate, conciliatory political culture as it allows candidates to get elected on a small percentage of the popular vote, and therefore encourages them to 'play to their base' (i.e. their core constituency). In their study on Northern Ireland's path to stability, Robin Wilson and Rick Wilford suggest the use of the quota means a candidate only requires approximately 14% of the vote to get elected. This means that he or she has no electoral incentive to reach out to undecided voters, or supporters of other parties. In their words, introducing STV has meant 'elections have become entirely communalised affairs, rewarding intra-ethnic outbidding as the only competition' ('Northern Ireland: a route to stability?' 2002).

- Although large by FPTP standards, STV constituencies tend to be much smaller than those used for list PR. This can lead to two significant problems. First, it can affect the proportionality of the result, since evidence suggests proportionality is determined as much by the size of constituency as by any other factor, including choice of electoral system. Second, it is more vulnerable to gerrymandering, where constituency boundaries are deliberately skewed to serve the interests of a particular individual or group.

- The use of hand-counting mechanisms with STV can lead to inaccuracies at each stage of the counting process. The experience of Northern Ireland and Scotland is that electronic counting is a necessary requirement. However, this can remove some of the transparency (and excitement) present in a traditional FPTP hand-count .

- It does not automatically provide a proportional result. Since STV allows voters to select individual candidates as well as parties, it could be argued that this is not the main purpose of the electoral system. However, it is still a useful criterion for assessing STV, particularly since many of its advocates trumpet its virtues on the basis of its ability to deliver a proportional outcome. In the 2009 European Parliament elections, Sinn Féin received almost 9.0% more votes than the third-placed party, the Ulster Unionist Party (UUP), yet both parties received one seat each. The UUP benefited

Chapter 4

even more in the 2007 Northern Ireland Assembly elections when it received fewer votes than the Social and Democratic Labour Party yet won more seats.

Additional member system (AMS)

The additional member system is used for the Scottish Parliament, Welsh Assembly and London Assembly elections.

How does AMS work?

Several varieties of AMS exist, but they are basically a combination of first-past-the-post and party list voting. The purpose is to retain the best features of FPTP while introducing proportionality between parties through party list voting.

AMS requires large multi-member constituencies, containing a mixture of constituency and list seats. This provides the voter with the opportunity to use two votes: one for the regional member, and one for the constituency representative. Box 4.1 explains how this works in one part of Scotland.

Box 4.1

Example of how AMS works in Scotland

Mr L. lives in the town of East Linton. At the last Scottish Parliament election in 2007, he was able to vote for his Member of the Scottish Parliament (MSP) for the constituency of East Lothian, and a regional MSP for South of Scotland.

The other eight constituencies in this region were Ayr; Carrick; Cumnock and Doon Valley; Clydesdale; Cunninghame South; Dumfries, Galloway and Upper Nithsdale; Roxburgh and Berwickshire; and Tweeddale, Ettrick and Lauderdale.

While the constituency of East Lothian elected a Labour MSP, the distribution of MSPs for the region of South of Scotland is: Labour five MSPs, Scottish National Party five MSPs, Conservatives four MSPs and Liberal Democrats two MSPs.

This system was introduced for the new regional assemblies in the UK after 1997. The Scottish Parliament is made up of 129 MSPs. There are currently 73 constituency MSPs and 56 regional list MSPs.

The Welsh National Assembly consists of 60 elected members, elected from five electoral regions: 40 are constituency Assembly Members and are voted for using FPTP, while the remaining 20 are elected using a list system.

The London Assembly consists of 25 members elected from 14 constituencies. The remaining 11 members are known as 'London-wide members', as they are elected by votes cast across the whole of the Greater London Authority area and thus do not represent any particular constituency.

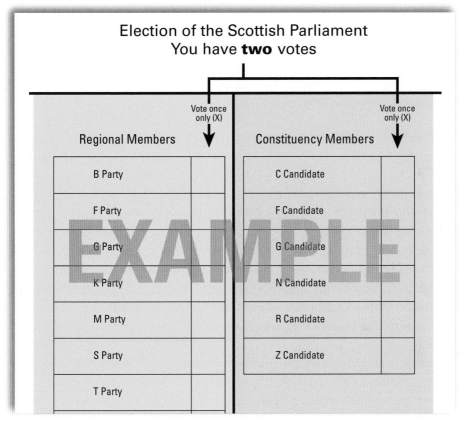

Figure 4.1 Sample AMS ballot paper for elections to the Scottish Parliament

As the sample Scottish Parliament ballot paper in Figure 4.1 illustrates, each voter has two votes: one vote for a single MP via FPTP and one for a regional or national party list. The balance between the constituency and list seats varies between countries: in Germany and New Zealand there is a straight 50:50 split, but in Scotland it is 55:45, and Wales 67:33. There are different ways for election officers to work out how many seats a party should have won, but in Scotland, London and Wales, the d'Hondt method is used:

- Step 1: count the total number of votes cast and divide it by the number of constituency seats won in the region plus 1 (this is sometimes called a party's 'average'). This means that parties which did not win a constituency seat are not discriminated against when the regional seats are distributed.

- Step 2: the party with the highest figure receives the first 'top-up' seat. If a party has been under-represented in the constituency vote, it is likely to receive more 'top-up' seats than a party which has benefited from the constituency vote.
- Step 3: the process is continued until all the 'top-up' seats in the region are filled. Each time a party receives a 'top-up' seat, its average changes.

Usually, certain criteria have to be met before a party is eligible for a 'top-up' seat. In Germany, a party must win either 5% of the total vote or at least one constituency seat. In this way, it is hoped to prevent extremist parties with little concentrated support from gaining representation.

What have been the main effects of using AMS in the UK?

- One of this system's advantages is that it offers greater voter choice. By 'splitting the ticket', voters can select a different party for their constituency and list votes. Evidence suggests that the electorates throughout the UK have quickly grasped how to maximise their preferences. It is estimated that 27% of Scottish voters and 20% of Welsh voters voted for different parties with their constituency and regional votes. This suggests that ticket-splitting is more likely to take place where there is a higher percentage of list MPs, indicating that voters have thought about how to maximise their votes under AMS.
- AMS generally increases the number of parties gaining representation. The composition of the Scottish Parliament after the 2003 elections included nine parties with MSPs, a figure that included two independents and five parties that were not represented at Westminster. The 2007 results produced a slightly different picture with a single independent and five parties winning seats. A similar picture has emerged in Wales, with four parties and a single independent represented in the assembly in Cardiff.
- While the extent of proportionality is largely dependent on the ratio of FPTP:PR, AMS has produced more proportional results than elections held under FPTP (see Figure 4.2). However, the link between electoral system and proportionality could be misleading. Some academics believe that constituency size has a bigger impact on proportionality than the type of system used. Research by Richard Katz on the effects of 'district magnitude' suggests that systems such as AMS lead to more proportional results because they include much larger constituencies in comparison to those used for plurality or majoritarian systems.

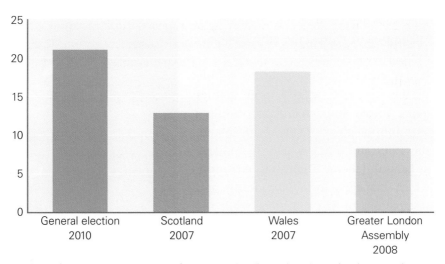

Note: figures measure deviation from proportionality against the regional votes only.

Figure 4.2 Deviation from proportionality of recent elections in the UK

- It has had a positive impact on voter turnout. Most studies on voter turnout argue that a range of factors influences the likelihood of an individual to vote. However, two of the most common factors are the impact that a person's vote is likely to have, and the sense that a genuine choice is offered by the parties standing for election. While it is difficult to establish a precise link between the type of electoral system used and increased turnout, the 'headline' figures indicate a positive correlation. Turnout has ranged between: 51% and 58% in Scotland (1999–2007); 38% and 43% in Wales; and 32% and 45% in London. In particular, turnout in the regional vote tended to be higher than for the constituency vote in London, perhaps hinting at the positive effects a proportional system can have on turnout.

- It has also led to greater representation of minorities. The Welsh Assembly became the first legislature in the world to have 50% women members after the elections in 2003. The following year, it became the first legislature to have a majority of women representatives when Trish Law won a by-election in Blaenau Gwent. The percentage of women representatives fell slightly in 2007 to 46.7%. Plaid Cymru has deliberately adapted its candidate selection procedures to exploit the opportunity for improving minority representation through AMS, by reserving the top place on each list for a woman. The list vote also allowed Glasgow to elect Scotland's first ethnic-minority MSP, Bashir Ahmad, as a list SNP MSP in Glasgow. Mr Ahmad's unique status in the Scottish Parliament, and the fact that only eight out of 25 Greater London Assembly members are women, suggests that changing the electoral system is perhaps of secondary importance when attempting to redress the ethnic balance of the UK's legislatures.

- It has created a new political culture in the devolved regions, with parties being forced into coalitions or ruling as minority governments. In Scotland, the 1999 and 2003 elections produced a Labour–Liberal Democrat coalition, which managed to survive deaths and resignations of first ministers, while the SNP (plus two Green MSPs) formed a minority administration in 2007. The effects of this new style of politics appear to have been largely positive, with the Liberal Democrats pushing Labour towards more innovative policy approaches, and coalition politics leading to a more consensual relationship with the other parties at Holyrood. Public opinion has been largely favourable: polling carried out by Johns and Carman ('Coping with coalitions? Scottish voters under a proportional system', 2008) suggested that a majority of Scottish voters preferred coalitions to single-party government (with the number growing since 1999).

Scottish National Party MSP Bashir Ahmad after taking the oath at the Scottish Parliament in Edinburgh

- Where there is a significant bias towards constituency seats, as is the case in Wales, it is more likely that a party can govern alone. After the 2003 Welsh Assembly elections, Labour decided it could do without a coalition partner as it had won 50% of the assembly seats.

- AMS also preserves some of the disadvantages of FPTP, for example, the problem of wasted votes in the constituency vote. A Labour supporter in Roxburgh and Berwickshire (Scotland) would be wasting his or her vote in a seat where the party has finished fourth in the last two Scottish Parliament elections.

- One significant problem with AMS experienced to varying degrees in Scotland, Wales and London is the relatively high number of spoilt ballot papers. In 2007 in Scotland, 3.5% of all ballot papers were rejected, with the number of rejected papers in Edinburgh Central outnumbering the size of the winning candidate's majority. The rise in the number of rejected ballots is largely attributable to two factors:

- First, the decision to hold Scottish local elections on the same day arguably created confusion in the minds of some voters as Scotland uses STV to elect its local councillors. Several reports suggest that it was a mistake to expect voters to be able to operate two very different systems at the same time
- Second, the ballot paper for AMS changed for 2007. In previous elections, two separate papers had been used: one for each of the two votes provided under AMS. It is possible that some voters only used one of the votes. By way of contrast, the number of rejected papers fell by 4.2% in the 2008 Greater London Assembly election, where the authorities decided to use two ballot papers instead of one.

- A problem common to all mixed member systems is that of the different status and role of constituency and list representatives. Since regional members have not been directly elected by the voters, and rely wholly on the patronage of the party leadership for their position in the list, they arguably lack the legitimacy of their directly-elected colleagues. This argument is enhanced when defeated candidates from constituency contests appear in the legislature courtesy of their ranking on the party lists. This issue was brought into sharp focus in Clwyd West in Wales in 2005. The defeated Conservative, Liberal Democrat and Plaid Cymru candidates in Clwyd West all happened to be elected via the regional list. In response to this particular case, the 2006 Government of Wales Act banned dual candidacy, ensuring that candidates could only appear on either the constituency or the regional ballot papers. Without a constituency to represent (or campaign in), list members can appear as though they lack a purpose in the legislature. In Wales, the response of Plaid Cymru to this situation has been to instruct some of its regional assembly members to open offices in the constituencies which they hope to fight in the next election and offer their services as 'alternative' assembly members to the electorate. Understandably, this has provoked considerable anger on the part of the elected assembly members in these constituencies.

Closed-list PR

Closed-list PR is used for European Parliament elections in Great Britain.

How does closed-list PR work?

There are many varieties of party list voting, but the most basic forms are the 'closed' and 'open' party list systems. Both systems require a multi-member constituency, which can, as with Israel, be a whole country. Under the **open list** system, which is found in countries such as Belgium and the Netherlands, voters are free to choose between voting for an individual candidate and simply voting for their favourite party.

The **closed list** system is more straightforward, with voters only having the option to choose between the respective parties (see Figure 4.3). After the votes have been counted, each party receives the same percentage of seats as votes received. Voters have advance knowledge of each party's rank order of candidates, and those candidates placed towards the top of their party's list stand a better chance of being elected than those lower down.

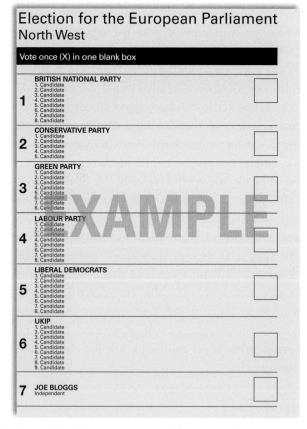

Figure 4.3 Sample ballot paper for the European Parliament elections in the North West region, 2009

In the UK, there are 12 European electoral regions, with each region having between three and ten MEPs. Each group of MEPs is responsible for representing the whole of that region.

The European Parliament in Strasbourg

What are the main effects of using closed-list PR?

- The most obvious effect is that a greater number of parties are able to win seats. Compared to FPTP in the 2010 general election, which resulted in candidates from six parties winning seats in mainland Britain, eight different parties won seats under closed-list PR in the 2009 European Parliament election.
- The European elections offered parties who have traditionally found it difficult or impossible to win seats at Westminster the opportunity for significant electoral success (see Table 4.3).

Table 4.3　Comparison of minor party electoral performance under FPTP and closed list

	MPs after 2010 general election	MEPs after 2009 European Parliament election
Greens	1	2
BNP	0	2
UKIP	0	13

- There are fewer wasted votes, as the d'Hondt seat allocation method allows parties receiving small numbers of votes to gain an MEP. It was estimated by the pro-reform pressure group Makemyvotecount after the June 2009 European Parliament election that at least 75% of voters were represented by at least one candidate from a party they voted for. In the South East, the proportion is almost 90%.
- As it is a purely proportional system, using large multi-member constituencies, it should guarantee a tight link between votes cast and seats won. However, as the results from the 2009 elections to the European Parliament illustrate, this is not always the case, with the cumulative DV of 13 appearing high for an election held under list PR (see Table 4.4). Even so, the use of list PR prevented some of the electoral distortions that would have occurred had FPTP been used instead. In the North East, for example, Labour might have won all the available seats under FPTP on 25% of the votes. Using list PR ensured that the three available seats were evenly distributed between Labour, the Conservatives and Liberal Democrats.

Table 4.4 Results of the UK European Parliament elections, 2009

	% votes	% seats	DV
Conservatives	28	35	+7
UKIP	17	18	+1
Labour	16	18	+2
Liberal Democrat	16	15	−1
Green	9	3	−6
BNP	6	3	−3
SNP	2	3	+1
Plaid Cymru	1	1	–
Others	9	4	−5

- With only a single 'X' to mark on the ballot paper, it is simple to use and easy to understand.
- Party lists ensure that women and members of minorities are elected in higher numbers, as party managers have a greater control over who is likely to be elected through their control of the list's rank order: 24/72 UK MEPS elected in 2009 are women, while 5.7% of UK MEPs are from a minority ethnic group, the highest total of any assembly elected from the UK apart from the Greater London Assembly.
- However, some critics of PR have suggested that a lack of understanding of how votes are translated into seats under the d'Hondt system undermines

the democratic credentials of closed-list PR. If voters do not understand the link between their 'X' and the election of an MEP, critics query how far it can claim to be a legitimate alternative to FPTP, which is transparent in its counting process and the link between vote and seat is easy to understand.

- Even allowing for the traditional indifference demonstrated by the UK electorate to 'second-order' elections, and to European Parliament elections in particular, the turnout in 2009 challenges the view that PR automatically boosts turnout. A total of 34.5% was down 5% on 2004, and even lower than the last election held under FPTP in 1994.

- The use of a closed list, where voters are only able to vote for parties rather than candidates, places tremendous power in the hands of party elites, who are responsible for placing their candidates in rank order. It also limits voter choice, and therefore risks adding to the alienation felt by some voters towards the political system.

- Perhaps most controversially, the 2009 election seemed to justify the warnings of anti-PR reformers who argue that PR allows extremist groups, such as the BNP, to gain representation. Under FPTP, the BNP would not have won any seats with 6% support. However, under closed-list PR, it was able to get two candidates elected. The experience of countries around the world which use PR might suggest that parties such as this could gain significant political influence should their support be necessary for a future PR-created coalition government to survive.

- It could also be said to render futile the campaigning of any candidate lower down the list and therefore unlikely to be elected. Beyond any benefit for their party in their region, such candidates received no direct benefit for their efforts.

Supplementary vote (SV)

This system was created by Labour MP Dale Campbell-Savours, and featured prominently in the Plant Report published by the Labour Party in 1993. As well as being used to elect the Mayor of London and mayors in 12 English towns, a variant of it is used to elect the Sri Lankan president. In this case, the voter can express three preferences as opposed to two. It also has much in common with the alternative vote, although voters express their preference with an 'X' rather than ranking candidates with numbers. (However, Newham adopted a numerical ranking system in 2006.)

How does SV work?

With this system, the voter is faced with two columns on the ballot paper. In the first column the first choice is indicated by marking an 'X', and in the second one the next preference is recorded in the same manner. Voters do not have to express a second preference if they do not wish to.

Election of the Mayor

Vote once (X) in column one for your first choice
Vote once (X) in column two for your second choice

			column one first choice	column two second choice
	1	BARNBROOK, Richard British National Party		
	2	BATTEN, Gerard Joseph UK Independence Party		
	3	BERRY, Sian Green Party		
	4	CRAIG, Alan Christian Peoples Alliance and Christian Party		
	5	GERMAN, Lindsey Ann Left List		
	6	JOHNSON, Boris Conservative Party		
	7	LIVINGSTONE, Ken The Labour Party Candidate		
	8	McKENZIE, Winston Truman Independent		
	9	O'CONNOR, Matt English Democrats - "Vote Matt! Vote English!"		
	10	PADDICK, Brian Leonard Liberal Democrats		

Figure 4.4 Ballot paper for the 2008 London Mayoral Election

If one candidate gets 50% of the first-preference vote, he or she is elected. If no candidate gains 50% of the vote, only the two most popular candidates go through to the next round, and the other candidates are eliminated. The second preferences of these candidates are then examined, and if they are for either of the two remaining candidates, their votes are transferred to those candidates. Whoever has the most votes at the end of the process is elected. An example is given in Table 4.5.

Table 4.5   Results of the London mayoral election, 2008

Candidate	1st Preferences	2nd Preferences	Total
Boris Johnson	1,043,761	124,977	1,168,738
Ken Livingstone	893,877	135,089	1,028,966
Brian Paddick	236,752		
Siân Berry	77,396		
Richard Barnbrook	69,753		
Alan Craig	39,266		
Gerard Batten	22,435		
Lindsey German	16,804		
Matt O'Connor	10,700		
Winston McKenzie	5,396		
Total	**2,415,958**		

What have been the main effects of using SV in the UK?

- Voter realisation that their vote is likely to affect the result, and the use of a competitive electoral system, suggest that SV can have a positive impact on turnout: 45% of Londoners turned out to vote in 2008. Turnout in Hackney in May 2010 was 58% — 1% higher than the turnout for the constituency of Hackney South and Shoreditch for the general election held on the same day.
- Few votes are wasted under SV. In 2008, 89.44% of Londoners who voted had one of their votes count in the final round.
- Votes can be wasted, however, if people do not vote for either of the two most popular candidates as first or second preferences. According to the Electoral Reform Society, 43.5% of second-preference votes in the 2005 Torbay mayoral election were wasted as they were not given to either of the top two candidates.
- Critics of SV argue that it is too complicated for some voters to understand, and therefore results in a significant number of unintentionally spoiled ballot papers. In the October 2005 mayoral election in Torbay, 1,750 of 24,500 ballot papers issued were spoiled. According to the Electoral Reform Society, this was either through a failure to understand the system, or because some voters did not nominate a second-preference candidate.
- Although it is a majoritarian system, SV is not guaranteed to provide the winning candidate with a majority of voters' first or second preferences. This is most likely to occur when voters do not select a second preference (18.43% voters did not express a second preference in London in 2008) or

when there are more than two strong candidates. In 2008, 47.57% of voters selected Boris Johnson for one of their preferences, while Ken Livingstone received 48.74% of first- and second-preference votes. Recent mayoral elections in English towns have illustrated this particular problem to an even greater extent. Peter Davies was elected mayor in Doncaster in 2009 with only 33% of the total vote, while Stuart Drummond's winning total of 32% in Hartlepool was even less impressive.

- A candidate is not assured of receiving a majority of the second-preference votes cast for him or her. Since only the second preferences of rejected candidates (i.e. those outside the top two) count, an election which sees many voters cast their preferences for the two most popular candidates is likely to deny the top two most of their preferences. For example in 2008, Boris Johnson gained 257,792 second-choice votes, but only 124,977 of them transferred to him in the second round, while Ken Livingstone gained 303,198 second-choice votes, but only 135,089 of them transferred to him in the second round.

- Ultimately, SV relies on an assumption that there will only be two candidates with a chance to win. The recent political experience of the UK illustrates that this is a flawed assumption. For example, the first and third placed-candidates were separated by only 1% in Doncaster, yet this made no difference to who went through to the redistributive stage.

Conclusion: has the use of different electoral systems strengthened the case for further electoral reform?

Although the UK's experiment with new methods of voting has thrown up some interesting and unexpected problems and outcomes, the experience overall has been largely positive. Whichever criterion one uses, whether it is proportionality, voter turnout, voter choice, government stability, or fair representation of minorities, the three proportional systems have fared as well as FPTP in each category, and in most cases produced even better results.

Some significant issues have arisen, chiefly over the 2007 elections in Scotland, but also concerning the role of party elites in selecting candidates. However, in the case of Scotland, the origins of these issues appear to be more to do with poor administration than any intrinsic fault with the electoral systems used. Where the role of party managers is concerned, the attitudes which limit the selection of more women and members of ethnic minorities have a much greater effect on minority representation under FPTP, and should, over time, become more sensitive in their approach.

The lessons learned from the UK's experience of a diverse electoral map depend to a large extent on the observer's attitude towards electoral reform in general. As a result, the degree to which this experience calls into question the future use of FPTP is open to interpretation.

Task 4.1

(In the style of AQA Unit 1: People, Politics and Participation)
Study Figure 4.2 on page 57.
1 Explain what is meant by the term 'deviation from proportionality'. *(5 marks)*
2 Using the source and your own knowledge, identify and explain two strengths of proportional systems which have been used in the UK since 1997. *(10 marks)*

Task 4.2

(In the style of OCR Unit F851: Contemporary Politics of the UK, Section A)
1 Why would some people claim that the UK's experience of proportional electoral systems has not been a success? *(30 marks)*

Guidance on how to approach these tasks is provided online at www.hodderplus.co.uk/philipallan.

Further reading

- Electoral Reform Society (2007) 'Britain's experience of electoral systems': http://tinyurl.com/2wrqxc6
- Ministry of Justice (2008) 'The experience of new voting systems in the United Kingdom since 1997': http://tinyurl.com/2sgv8u
- Rallings & Thrasher (2008) 'London Mayor and Assembly Elections 2008: Report to the Electoral Commission': http://tinyurl.com/3abv3xf

What factors influence the way people vote?

One of the attractions of studying voting behaviour, or **psephology**, is that it focuses on how and why ordinary people interact with the political process. What is it that prompts someone to place their cross next to the name of a particular candidate? In the pre-democratic age — that is, until the introduction of the mass franchise and, crucially, the secret ballot in 1872 — the answer to this question would have been a lot simpler. Bribery, fear and alcoholic inducements would all have played a significant part in explaining election results.

However, as political parties and the electorate grew in tandem, it became considerably more difficult to explain the fortunes of parties at general elections. What is surprising, therefore, is that the first major academic study of voting behaviour was not published until shortly after the Second World War. Since that time, various theories or models of voting behaviour have been put forward. This chapter explains each of the main theories in turn, and evaluates critically how relevant they are in explaining both why individuals vote in the way they do, and the results of recent general elections.

How far do social factors influence voting behaviour?

The earliest studies of how people voted all highlighted the importance of particular social characteristics in influencing the voter's actions at the ballot box. That is to say, people identified themselves with a particular social group, and voted for the party that they felt was best able to meet the demands of that group. Although this behaviour is difficult to analyse accurately, academics were led to conclude that voters saw themselves as part of a group, and were either able to recognise common group interests or sufficiently influenced by their family members and workmates to vote in a certain direction.

A person's class, age, religion, or gender therefore all had a strong influence. However, most studies until the mid-1970s emphasised the importance of **class** as the most significant social influence on voting.

Class

The era of alignment

The starting point for any explanation of the role of class in influencing voting behaviour has to be Butler and Stokes' classic work *Political Change in Britain* (1969). This laid down an analysis which is the basis of all argument on how people vote.

The core of their argument is as follows:

- Voters can identify one party as representing the interests of a particular class (Labour for the working class and the Conservatives for the middle class).
- Voters do not believe that 'their' party is necessarily hostile to other classes; in other words, by voting for that party they believe that they are acting in the much broader national interest.
- Loyalty to that party does not automatically originate in approval for that party's policies, merely in a belief that this is what someone from that class should do. Thus, a welder from the North East might vote Labour because that is what most other manual workers from that region do.
- Voters are significantly influenced by their parents and their peers (a process known as **socialisation**) into supporting one party, and align themselves with this party for most of their lifetime. This process of party identification is dealt with in greater detail later in the chapter.

At the time, there was ample evidence to support this viewpoint. The UK had a strong two-party system, with little political instability. In an era of relatively low social mobility, both Labour and Conservative parties dominated UK politics and enjoyed a roughly equal share of power between 1945 and 1979. Studies of how manual (Labour) and non-manual (Conservative) workers voted, strongly backed up Butler and Stokes' argument.

How relevant is this argument in the modern political age? As will be demonstrated later, Butler and Stokes' model has been exposed to some harsh criticism. However, the evidence from the last two general elections offers some support for the view that class is still an influential determinant of electoral behaviour, even if it can probably no longer be viewed as the single most influential factor (see Tables 5.1 and 5.2). Interestingly, the Conservatives were the largest party among the ABC1 groups in 2010, which comprise the bulk of the electorate and the social groups most likely to vote. In short, class was important in 2010 because the Conservatives won most of the votes of their natural supporters, and they turned out in greater numbers than any other social group.

Table 5.1 Breakdown of the 2005 general election results by social class (change from 2001 in brackets)

Party	AB (%) Higher/intermediate professional, managerial and administrative	C1 (%) Supervisory, clerical and other non-manual	C2 (%) Skilled manual	DE (%) Semi- and unskilled manual/ casual workers, people reliant on state benefits
Labour	28 (–2)	32 (–6)	40 (–9)	48 (–7)
Conservative	37 (–2)	36 (—)	33 (+4)	25 (+1)
Liberal Democrat	29 (+4)	23 (+3)	19 (+4)	18 (+5)
Others	6	9	8	9

Table 5.2 Breakdown of the 2010 general election results by social class (change from 2005 in brackets)

Party	AB	C1	C2	DE
Conservative	39 (+2)	39 (+3)	37 (+4)	31 (+6)
Labour	26 (–2)	28 (–4)	29 (–11)	40 (–8)
Liberal Democrat	29	24 (+1)	22 (+3)	17 (–1)
Others	7 (+1)	9	12 (+4)	12 (+3)

Source: How Britain voted in 2010 (Ipsos-MORI) (**www.ipsos-mori.com**)

How has the class-based approach to explaining voting behaviour been criticised?

A more convincing analysis of the last two general elections would argue that the class-based model of voting behaviour is no longer credible, as there has been a pronounced decline in the levels of absolute and relative class-based voting (see Box 5.1). Not only are voters more willing to vote for a party that does not 'represent' their particular class, but voters, in general, are less predictable in their voting patterns.

Box 5.1

Absolute and relative class voting

Absolute class voting = proportion of middle class voting Conservative + proportion of the working class voting Labour

Relative class voting = % working class voting Labour – % middle class voting Labour

Why is class no longer the key determinant of voting behaviour?

- A significant amount of 'cross-class' voting has always taken place, with approximately one-third of working-class voters voting Conservative even during the high-point of the two-party system.
- Some sociologists dispute whether broad social categorisations such as class have any relevance in a modern, post-industrialised society, and would therefore deny any link between a person's membership of a social group and his or her political behaviour.
- The profound impact of deindustrialisation during the 1980s threw class-based analysis into turmoil as cleavages developed within the working class. As well as the stereotypical unionised manual worker, there was a proliferation of non-unionised clerical workers in the burgeoning service sector. Some commentators argue that it then became impossible to talk about a common class interest among the working class. A longer-term consequence of this has been the decline in the number of people who feel that they belong to a particular class.

Class dealignment

A more fundamental explanation for the decline in class-based voting has been provided by class dealignment theory. By the mid-1970s, the stable electoral landscape began to take on a very different form: first, support for the two main parties began to ebb away; second, the volatility of the electorate increased. That is to say, voters no longer felt as attached, or aligned, to a single party.

One important effect of dealignment on the political parties is that more voters are inclined to cast their vote for an increasingly diverse range of parties. While the extent of Liberal Democrat support has increased since 1979, so too has support for independent, local and marginal parties. One only has to consider the success of Martin Bell at Tatton in 1997, Dr Richard Taylor in Wyre Forest (2001 and 2005) and George Galloway's Respect Party (2005) to find evidence of this phenomenon.

The second significant impact of dealignment has been to increase the volatility of the electorate, creating a group of voters whose political preferences cannot be banked on by any of the parties and who are thus more susceptible to the shorter-term influences of the election campaign. The size of this group of voters has increased significantly during the era of dealignment. Bob Worcester of the polling organisation Ipsos-MORI estimated that there were approximately 900,000 floating voters in 2010.

Causes of class dealignment

Class dealignment can be explained by a number of factors.

- The long-standing period of deindustrialisation and industry's gradual replacement by a service-dominated economy has had profound social implications. One immediate consequence has been the reduction in the number of manual workers, partially due to the decline in the manufacturing sector, but also to the greater accessibility of higher education.

- Increasing voter awareness of differences between parties, and less reliance on emotive attachment to one party, has been facilitated by more people staying on beyond the minimum school-leaving age and subsequently going on to university.

- Another school of thought explains this process by examining structural cleavages within the working class, in particular whether or not workers rely on the public sector for the majority of their services. These might typically include housing, employment, benefits and transport. While these voters would be more likely to vote Labour, members of the working class who were able to 'consume' the majority of their services from the private sector would be more inclined to vote for the Conservatives. This analysis can be broadened to take into account other cleavages, such as union/non-union employment and North/South residence.

- A further explanation, which is also related to 'post-industrial' changes', relates to the way that people identify themselves. This has changed markedly during the last 20 years, with increased numbers of voters making their political preferences on the basis of a different form of social identification, such as gender, race, or age.

- Labour's abandonment of its traditional ideas and beliefs such as nationalisation, opposition to EU membership and redistributive economics has weakened the party's link with its core voters.

- The increase in support for the Liberal Democrats and regional nationalist parties has drawn voters from all social classes away from the 'big two'.

- Changing voter values has also been a significant factor. The increasing importance of 'post-material' issues, such as the environment, has drawn voters towards single-issue parties or candidates, and, to some extent has led to voters abandoning party politics altogether and using interest groups as a means of engaging with the political process instead.

- An interesting argument is put forward by Weakliem and Heath, in a chapter from *The End of Class Politics? Class Voting in Comparative Context* (1999). Disputing the causes provided above, the authors' main explanation is that dealignment has been a result of a slow, but steady, deterioration in public confidence in the government. This is why the main victim of dealignment in the UK has been the Labour Party, as it is the party most in favour of government intervention.

How has the class dealignment approach to explaining voting behaviour been criticised?

However, there remains considerable disagreement over the extent to which dealignment has taken place. Some argue that there is no empirical evidence for it at all, and claim that supporters of the dealignment thesis have been led towards an incorrect analysis because of the means of classification that they use. Goldthorpe, for example, rejects the manual/non-manual descriptors, offering as an alternative a model that focuses on whether someone is an employer, employee or self-employed, and the type of contract he or she is employed on (see Box 5.2).

Box 5.2

The Goldthorpe model of classification

I   Service class — higher-grade professionals, administrators, officials, managers, proprietors of moderate to big businesses

II   Service class — lower-grade professionals, administrators, officials, managers

III   Routine non-manual workers

IV   Small proprietors, self-employed, farmers

V   Lower-grade technicians, supervisors of manual workers

VI   Skilled manual workers

VII   Semi-skilled and unskilled manual workers

Weakliem and Heath suggest that the link between class and voting is largely influenced by attitudes towards the role of government, rather than the growth of post-materialism, better education or changes on party policies. As a result, they argue, the decline has not been as pronounced as others have previously suggested and is not necessarily permanent.

Finally, there is some merit in the argument that it is the changing size of the middle and working classes, and the differences in their likelihood to turn out, rather than the desertion of the working class that explains Labour's steady decline in its share of the vote. Put simply, the falling Labour share of the vote is largely due to the fact that a smaller number of the party's natural voters are prepared to vote.

Gender

Until 1997, the accepted wisdom was that women were, politically at least, far more conservative than men. However, following a pattern that has emerged in the USA since 1992, the direction of the female vote has changed: in each election since 1997, the Labour Party has benefited from the women's vote. In a study of global trends of how women voted, Pippa Norris and Ronald Inglehart linked these electoral changes to changes in women's levels of education and the extent to which they were in employment. These findings were borne out by a British Social Attitudes survey, which indicated that middle- and high-income women were more likely to vote Labour than their male counterparts. Evidence for this was provided by the result of the 2005 general election in which Labour received a clear majority of the female vote.

However, Labour's advantage among women did not last long. As Table 5.3 demonstrates, by 2010 it had suffered a significant reverse among female voters. This was, to some extent, a vindication of David Cameron's decision to specifically target female voters after being elected Conservative Party leader in 2005.

Table 5.3	Gender and voting in 2010

	Men	Women
Conservatives	38%	36%
Labour	38%	31%
Liberal Democrats	22%	26%

On the face of it, the evidence from 2010 seems to indicate that the significant swing among women voters away from Labour was an important factor in the election. If one explores a little deeper, and looks at the behaviour of women across the age ranges and class divisions, an interesting picture emerges (see Tables 5.4 and 5.5).

Table 5.4	The impact of women on the 2010 election result, with age considered (% men in brackets)

	Women 18–24 Turnout: 39% (50%)	Women 25–34 Turnout: 54% (56%)	Women 35–54 Turnout: 67% (67%)	Women 55+ Turnout: 73% (76%)
Conservatives	30 (29)	27 (42)	33 (36)	42 (41)
Labour	28 (34)	38 (23)	31 (28)	30 (29)
Liberal Democrats	34 (27)	27 (30)	29 (23)	21 (16)

Source: How Britain voted in 2010 (Ipsos-MORI) (www.ipsos-mori.com)

	Women AB Turnout: 39% (75%)	Women C1 Turnout: 54% (66%)	Women C2 Turnout: 67% (58%)	Women DE Turnout: 73% (56%)
Conservatives	34 (44)	39 (40)	41 (33)	29 (32)
Labour	29 (23)	28 (28)	25 (33)	45 (35)
Liberal Democrats	31 (27)	25 (22)	25 (19)	19 (13)

Table 5.5 The impact of women on the 2010 election result, with social class considered (% men in brackets)

Source: How Britain voted in 2010 (Ipsos-MORI) (**www.ipsos-mori.com**)

The data show how the support of women voters, in particular those sub-groups which turned out in greater numbers, may well have been an important factor in explaining Cameron's relative success on 6 May 2010: women aged 55+; women ABC1. They also suggest that the Conservatives had succeeded in bucking the trend of recent elections in winning the majority of younger female voters, while maintaining a clear lead among women voters aged 55+.

Box 5.3

2010: the mumsnet election?

Perhaps the ultimate compliment to the power of the female vote was paid by both main parties which, independently, took out paid adverts on the parenting website mumsnet.

According to one Labour strategist, there was political capital to be made by targeting voters in this way. Kerry McCarthy claimed mumsnet users were 'political animals, in that they are very interested in issues that affect their families and lives, but wouldn't necessarily watch *Newsnight* every night'.

However, the importance of the female vote can be qualified in three ways:
- While women certainly did not like Brown as leader, and were clearly sceptical about Labour's merits in general, this did not lead to a comparable swing to the Conservative Party. The increase in support from men and women 2005–10 for the Conservatives was 4%.
- A survey of women voters for the Fawcett Society in 2008 found that in answer to the question, 'Which political party, if any, do you think would be the best at looking after the interests of women?', the majority of respondents believed that it was the Labour Party, with 25% of female respondents making this choice. By way of comparison, 21% of female respondents believed that the Conservative Party would be the best at looking after women's interests. This is significant as it suggests that women's

political choices are not necessarily tied to who they believe will best look after their gender's interests, and that other factors must therefore be more influential.

● It is a mistake to group all women together as a single entity. Survey data suggest that women are as likely as men to be influenced by other social factors, issues, the media or the performance of party leaders. For example, if one looks closely at the behaviour of women across the generations one will see that their behaviour follows similar patterns to that of their male counterparts across the age range, i.e. older voters are more likely to vote Conservative than their younger counterparts. This was certainly true among women in the 2010 election: 42% of women over the age of 55 voted Conservative (41% of men) compared to 30% (29% of men) who voted for the Labour Party. What this might suggest, therefore, is that age is a more influential determinant of voting behaviour than gender.

Age

'Young people can afford to be radical', 'socialism is something that you'll grow out of' and other such clichés have passed into popular folklore. But, given that there is an element of truth in most clichés, perhaps there is something in the view that the young tend to cast their vote for more left-wing groups and then move further to the right as they get older. Certainly evidence from the 2005 and 2010 elections would bear this out (see Table 5.6).

Table 5.6 Voting patterns according to age, 2005 and 2010

	2005			**2010**		
	Con	Lab	Lib Dem	Con	Lab	Lib Dem
18–24	28	38	26	30 (+2)	31	30
25–34	25	38	27	35 (+10)	30	29
35–44	27	41	23	34 (+7)	31	26
45–55	31	35	23	34 (+3)	28	26
55–64	39	31	22	38 (–1)	28	23
65+	38	31	15	41 (+3)	29	16

In 2005, among all voters aged 18–54, Labour enjoyed a clear majority over each of the other parties, while voters aged 55+ were considerably more likely to vote for the Conservative Party. By 2010, the situation had changed, with the Conservatives enjoying a majority of support across all ages, except the 18–24 bracket. Even so, the extent of direct transference from Labour to Conservatives seems quite small, with support for the Conservatives increasing at approximately the same rate as it does for the Liberal Democrats in all but the 25–34 and 35–44 age ranges.

Where the Conservative advantage does pay off, however, is in the 55–64 and 65+ age ranges where the party holds the biggest leads over the other two parties. These are the age ranges where turnout was highest, thus ensuring that the dominance of the Conservative party among voters aged 55+ was especially significant.

Region

During the 1980s, where voters lived was presented as a serious contender as the dominant social influence on voting. Indeed, the migration of workers from urban to rural communities, and from north to south, threatened to keep Labour in opposition almost permanently. However, this interpretation was challenged by those who felt that regional factors only really represented existing divisions between classes — for example voters in Wales tended to support the Labour Party because the country contained several large-scale industries, rather than because they lived in Wales. The sequence of Labour victories from 1997 to 2005 also raised questions about the importance of region as a significant factor, as the party managed to penetrate the bastions of Conservative support in the Midlands and South East.

The 2010 election largely confirmed the belief that where you live is not likely to act as a key determinant factor in how you vote, and that the patterns of support which emerged across the country are more likely to be a result of other factors.

The 2010 electoral map

To a certain extent, the electoral map returned to the picture it presented before Labour's 1997 landslide:
- The Conservatives became the largest single party in England, winning 39.5% of the vote and 56% of the seats.
- Labour's vote fell 7.4% to 28.1%, which brought it 36.1% of the seats.
- The Liberal Democrat vote increased 1.3%, but it lost four seats.

Labour's abject performance was highlighted by its loss of support in its traditional heartlands, such as the North East, where its vote fell to 43.6% — the first time it has ever fallen below 50%. Even so, a combination of the electoral system and a failure to capitalise by the other main parties came to

Labour's rescue, as it still managed to win 25/29 seats. The real losses came in the battleground constituencies of the Midlands, the Eastern counties and London, where Labour lost 56 seats directly to the Conservatives.

The picture in Scotland was very different; here the Conservatives achieved their third-lowest share of the vote since 1945, and only won a single seat (Dumfriesshire, Clydesdale and Tweeddale). In stark contrast to its performance in England, Labour managed to increase its share of the vote in Scotland, winning 42%, of the vote and 69% of seats. In the light of Labour's strong performance in Scotland, it is unsurprising that neither the SNP nor Liberal Democrats was able to make much of an impact. The SNP achieved a lower share of the vote than in the 1992, 1997 and 2001 elections, while the Liberal Democrats also fell back in terms of votes.

Wales provided a real break with past elections. The Conservative total of eight seats matches its 1987 achievement and it managed to take four seats from Labour. Its share of the vote was higher than any general election since 1992. Labour endured a torrid night. Although it was the largest party, with 36.3% of the vote, this figure was lower than in any general election since the First World War. The Liberal Democrats suffered at the hands of the electoral system as they achieved their second highest share of the vote since 1945, yet lost a seat to their 2005 total of four.

While Northern Ireland did not return any MPs for the main UK parties, it did throw up two interesting features. First, David Cameron's experiment of fielding joint Conservative-Ulster Unionist candidates failed miserably. The UUP lost its only MP, Lady Sylvia Hermon, as she defected in protest at the 'alliance' to run as an independent in North Down. She won, with 63.3% support. Second, Sinn Féin's vote increased to 25.5%, making it the largest party for the first time in the province's history.

Conclusion

Regional factors do not appear to have a huge impact on how a person votes, with the possible exception of Scotland, where the anti-Conservative mood seems ingrained in the political culture. However, the performance of the main parties in the different parts of the UK does go some way to explaining the overall result. The collapse of Labour's vote in England essentially gave the Conservatives their relative election success on 6 May, and while Labour has some serious thinking to do about its electoral strategy in England, it must be of some concern to the Conservative leadership that they were unable to make significant inroads into Labour strongholds in the northern English cities or anywhere in Scotland.

Party identification and voting behaviour

A more refined version of the class model of voting was offered by academics from Michigan State University in the 1960s. For this reason, the partisan identification model is often referred to as the 'Michigan model'. Like the class model, it emphasises the importance of 'irrational' influences on a voter's actions. It argues that voters base their choice on a long-term commitment to a party, and pay comparatively little attention to the policy differences between the parties at election time or the performance of the parties since the last election.

What is the extent and importance of party identification in the UK?

Until the mid-1970s, it was possible to argue two things about party identification: first, the vast majority of the country 'identified' with a political party, and second, nearly all of them identified with either the Labour or Conservative parties. This meant that very few uncommitted or 'floating' voters existed.

Most studies accept that the majority of the electorate still identifies with one or other of the major parties. However, there are three significant differences in the way people relate to the Labour and Conservative parties — differences that go some way to explaining the sequence of unusual election results in the UK since 1992:

- *Fewer* people claim to identify with one of the two major parties. Data from the 2010 British Election Study suggest that 57% of voters do so.
- The *extent* of identification has weakened quite dramatically since the 1960s, when around 40% of those eligible to vote were happy to be categorised as having a very strong identification with Labour or Conservative. The 2008 British Social Attitudes Survey, published in January 2010, found that only 17% of people who identified with a party had a strong identification with that party.
- Bucking the trend of the 1970s and 1980s, in recent years the Conservatives appear to have suffered a greater haemorrhaging of 'identifiers' than Labour, and the party failed to capitalise on the (small) weakening of identification with Labour between 2005 and 2010.

In spite of this, the weakening of identification has not had a decisive impact on the two-party system of government, as no other party has come close to challenging the ability of the 'big two' to win power.

However, while overall levels of support for the major parties have remained reasonably stable, voters have become more volatile in their electoral behaviour, and consequently shown a greater willingness to fluctuate between parties. As the number of seats that changed hands between Labour and the Conservatives in 2010 illustrates, voters are more willing to make bigger ideological leaps, trans-ferring their allegiance from the Conservatives to Labour in 1997, and back again in 2010.

Weakening of identification has also led to major changes in the UK political landscape. The most obvious impact has been the introduction of coalition politics at Westminster, alongside a notable increase in parliamentary representation for the Liberal Democrats, the election of the first Green MP, and the success of the independents mentioned earlier in this chapter.

Caroline Lucas became the Green Party's first MP at the 2010 general election

What factors have contributed to weakening partisanship?

The weakening of party identification in the UK has been caused by several factors.

Performance of the parties and their leaders

Underpinning voters' partisanship is a belief that their preferred party will ultimately implement the policies that will benefit them. It goes without saying that this attachment will be eroded if they lose faith in the ability of their party to represent their interests effectively.

The most extreme example of a government being on the receiving end of public disdain was between 1992 and 1997, when John Major's government recorded approval levels of just 15% at its point of lowest popularity. The

Conservatives failed to make a better impression when in opposition after 1997, and even the Blair government, with three successive election victories, could not claim to enjoy huge amounts of public confidence. The 2001 victory was achieved with a record low turnout, and in 2005 the party retained power with only 35% of the popular vote. Its defeat in 2010 saw it achieve 29%, the party's second-lowest total since 1918.

Ideological disjuncture

During the golden era of partisanship, both main parties remained true to a broadly consistent ideological package. One explanation for weakening partisanship is that both parties moved away from their core support, and as a consequence undermined the attachment felt by their partisan supporters. For Labour, this process occurred during the early 1980s, when the party lurched to the left under the leadership of Michael Foot. The Conservative Party, too, was also guilty of moving away from its traditional voter base by the end of its 18-year period in office. This was, in part, because of public unrest at the less palatable effects of the government's privatisation programme, and a feeling that institutions such as the NHS were being undermined by creeping privatisation.

The impact of the media

While it is very difficult to draw a direct line between increasing media attention to political life and weakening partisanship, it does not require a huge leap of faith to accept that the more we learn about parties and politicians, the more likely we are to question long-held preconceptions and attitudes. This is especially true when one takes into account the increasingly critical approach of the media to politicians on all sides, and the cynicism towards public figures that this engenders.

To what extent is issue voting important?

In the 1950s electoral studies were revolutionised by the work of Anthony Downs. He did not agree with the view that voters based their electoral preferences on long-term sociological factors, or indeed that a high level of party identification still existed. Instead, he argued that voters treated political parties in the same way that they treated consumer goods, and therefore based their choice at election time on the likely 'costs' or 'benefits' of voting for a particular party.

Although some undecided voters might have paid attention to campaigns and policy positions during the era of alignment, the impact of issues was only felt to be short-term and partial. However, as the electoral landscape changed, and evidence emerged about the decline of class and partisan alignment, **rational voting** appeared to offer a more credible explanation for electoral behaviour.

The spatial model

In his original study, Downs argued that parties that avoided extreme positions on the majority of issues would appeal to the highest number of voters. His conclusion, therefore, was that a successful party had to position itself in the middle ground of a left–right political spectrum, in order to avoid alienating large numbers of possible supporters. This would appear to have been borne out by the failure of the Labour Party to win power in the 1980s, with an agenda that was regarded as too 'socialist' by the electorate, and by the Conservatives' failure between 1997 and 2010. The Conservative Party was seen as moving too far to the right in an attempt to distinguish itself from a centrist Labour Party. While the Conservative Party succeeded in stabilising its core vote in 2001 and 2005, it still failed to broaden its appeal beyond its natural supporters. This was a lesson that the Conservatives had learned by 2010, when their entire campaign was focused on a centrist approach.

This 'spatial model' of voting (so called because parties have to occupy the median space on a left–right political spectrum) has been criticised for offering an outdated and overly simplistic analysis.

The valence model

An alternative model of issue voting is the valence model. It argues that voter choice is based on an evaluation of partisan attachment, leader images and parties' actual and anticipated performance on valence issues — issues that are more general and virtually uncontested. Examples of valence issues might be 'prosperity', 'safer streets', 'successful schools' and 'national security'. Bob Worcester, founder of MORI, offers a refined version of this model, referring instead to 'the political triangle' of leader image, party image and issues.

Ultimately, the great strength of the valence model of issue voting is that it factors in a range of long- and short-term influences on electoral behaviour. Worcester's version is especially useful as it attempts to weigh up the relative importance of the three elements of the political triangle. For 2010, MORI estimated that the relative weightings were:

- leader image   39% (+8% from 2005)
- issues   39% (−6% from 2005)
- party image   22% (−2% from 2005)

Data from the 2010 British Election Study (BES) suggest that where 'leader image' was concerned, Gordon Brown had a very low approval rating at the start of the campaign, and his performance during the campaign failed to improve his ratings. Indeed, most voters had already made up their minds about him even before the Gillian Duffy incident in Rochdale. Meanwhile, public opinion on David Cameron and Nick Clegg was divided. The BES found that Clegg was liked by most voters, and was felt to have run the best campaign. On the other hand, Cameron was consistently felt to be the best potential prime minister. The public perception of the leaders was partially influenced by the leadership debates — Clegg received the largest boost to his approval ratings from these. Gordon Brown's low ratings appeared to reflect both public scepticism about his competence and his low levels of popularity.

Where Labour enjoyed leads on the major issues in 1997, 2001 and 2005, no single party enjoyed a clear lead on the most important issues in 2010. The economy was, by some distance, the most important issue for voters during the election, but the BES found that only 1% separated 'no party', 'the Conservatives', and 'Labour' as being the best on the most important issue. This might seem surprising during a period when the UK economy was facing its worst crises for 60 years, but the Conservatives' decision to focus on government debt possibly backfired, as did their emphasis on austerity measures to tackle the country's economic problems.

Advocates of the valence issue model would argue that this approach accurately explains the result of the 2010 election, since no single party was able to gain a lead in each of the two campaign elements of the model, while the impact of partisan dealignment on the two main parties was broadly similar.

To what extent does tactical voting affect the results of general elections?

Tactical or 'insincere' voting takes place when a supporter of a party with little chance of winning a constituency transfers his or her vote to another party in an attempt to prevent the leading party from winning the seat again. A good example of this in action is provided in Table 5.7, which gives the results for the constituency of Cheadle in Cheshire, 1997–2010, and demonstrates the impact of Labour voters switching tactically to the Liberal Democrats. While the size of the Conservative vote has not fluctuated significantly, the fall in vote share for Labour during this period, particularly in 2001 and 2005, has helped the Liberal Democrats to win and defend the seat.

| Table 5.7 | Parliamentary election results (%) for Cheadle constituency, 1997–2010 |

	1997	2001	2005	2005 by-election	2010
Conservative	43.7	42.3	40.4	42.4	40.8
Liberal Democrat	37.7	42.4	48.9	52.2	47.1
Labour	15.7	14.0	8.8	4.64	9.4

Tactical voting has grown in popularity and significance since the early 1990s, when it became clear that the swing to Labour was greatest in Conservative/Labour marginals. According to Professor John Curtice, tactical voting was worth 20 seats to Labour in 1997, and a further 12 to the Liberal Democrats. Dr Stephen Fisher estimates that its importance has now grown to the point where approximately 40 seats are affected by tactical voting.

Influences on the decision to vote tactically can be diverse. Usually, one assumes that a willing tactical voter is aware of the national situation and of the impact that a favourable result in his or her constituency will have on the final outcome of the election. Typically, a tactical voter will support a third-placed party, have a link to one of the other parties and possess a strong antipathy towards the other major party in the constituency.

How has the operation of tactical voting developed in recent years?

The working of tactical voting has changed in several ways:
- The Conservatives are no longer the only target of tactical voters.
- It could be argued that the purpose of tactical voting has subtly changed. In 2005, the electorate seemed capable of using this procedure to deliver a 'bloody nose' to Tony Blair's government, that is, keeping him in power, but with a much reduced majority. The Labour vote fell most sharply in its own seats, with the Liberal Democrats appearing to be the prime beneficiaries where they had previously lain second to Labour.

- Voters have demonstrated a greater willingness to organise tactical voting on a mass scale and across different constituencies. In 2005, a number of websites advocated 'voteswapping', although the impact of such sites was not thought to be significant.
- Some candidates decided to drop out of the 2010 election altogether to increase the chances for other candidates. The Green candidate for Weston-super-Mare, Dr Richard Lawson, pulled out, advising his supporters to vote Liberal Democrat, but in spite of his efforts, the Conservatives retained the seat.
- Senior Labour figures, including Ed Balls and Peter Hain, advised voters in constituencies where the Liberal Democrats were the main rivals to vote tactically.
- David Cameron's efforts to rebrand the Conservative party may have weakened the likelihood of tactical voting, as wavering Liberal Democrats, who might have voted tactically to keep Labour in power from 1997, might have been less frightened by the prospect of a Conservative government and voted Liberal Democrat instead. This was borne out by evidence from the election, as the number of Liberal Democrat voters intending to vote tactically fell significantly from 2005 (see Box 5.4).

Box 5.4

Tactical voting by Liberal Democrat supporters, 1997–2010

In response to a MORI poll asking:

Which of the following comes closest to your reasons for intending to vote for the party...?

1 It is the party that most represents your views.

OR

2 The party you support has little chance of winning in this constituency so you vote for xxx party to try to keep another party out.

The response from Liberal Democrat voters 1997–2010 clearly indicates a changed approach. The proportion of Liberal Democrat supporters agreeing with the second reason for voting for xxx party was:

- 1997   21%
- 2001   25%
- 2005   20%
- 2010   16%

- Even so, sufficient numbers of Liberal Democrat and Labour voters voted tactically to prevent a complete Conservative victory. In the South West, for example, Labour's share of the vote fell 7.4% to 15.4%, its lowest total in any region. Although the Conservative vote increased 4.2%, and they managed to win 11 seats, the Liberal Democrat vote also increased 2.2%, and they only lost 3 seats. There is reasonably strong evidence, therefore, that tactical voting by Labour voters managed to limit Conservative advances in the South West, to the benefit of the Liberal Democrats.
- Widespread tactical voting was arguably the main reason why the Conservative Party failed to win any of its 11 'target' seats in Scotland. In Perth and North Perthshire, the SNP candidate asked Labour voters to 'lend' him their votes: his majority tripled, and in several other constituencies, including former chancellor Alastair Darling's seat in Edinburgh South West, incumbent Labour MPs increased their majorities.

Conclusion: why do we vote the way we do?

For all the theories, data analysis and new interpretations, the last 30 years have seen relative consistency in the factors that most influence how we vote. Given the post-industrial splintering of the working class, it has become increasingly difficult to discuss the leaning of that particular class in any meaningful sense. When one also considers the deliberate repositioning of that social group's 'natural' party, it could be seen as quaintly old-fashioned to link Labour closely with any form of manual or low-paid work.

For all the interest they generate, other social factors lack the distinctive influence to be regarded as significant. While the rise of New Labour coincided with the changing direction of the female vote, this appears to have been a temporary phenomenon, and has largely been offset by the ageing nature of the UK's population — a development that most benefits the Conservative Party. What has changed, though, is the balance between different sectors of the population among those who actually turn out to vote. In 2010 pre-campaign polling suggested that older, more middle-class voters were more likely to vote than any other groups. As this section of the electorate is more inclined towards the Conservatives, a defeat for Gordon Brown was always on the cards.

Does this mean that we are all cold, analytical, rational voters, then? Here too, there are problems. It is difficult to equate an electorate that shows decreasing interest in all forms of political communication, coupled with an ambivalent approach to voting, with one that has a firm grasp of issue salience, can distinguish between different policy standpoints and can then vote for the party most closely positioned to its own. Fundamentally, it assumes a level of voter interest and sophistication that the evidence suggests is markedly absent.

Ultimately, the electorate is a sophisticated beast, able to balance longer-term affiliations and values with short-term trends and events. The story of the 2010 election was one where most voters had, at best, a weak affiliation to any political party, but no single party was able to fully exploit the opportunities created by declining levels of identification.

Task 5.1

(In the style of AQA Unit 1: People, Politics and Participation)

Source A

Tactical voting works at last

The story of this election is that both the Labour and the Lib Dem vote held up remarkably well in their respective strongholds, thereby blocking the Tory advance in two key battleground regions.

Labour's electoral strategy ultimately came down to defending seats in its core areas of support. While Labour was never going to be facing electoral melt-down on the scale of the Tories in 1997, nobody had predicted that the Labour vote would have held up quite as well as it did, particularly in Scotland and in North West England — with the latter proving a crucial element in preventing a Conservative majority.

The list of seats which the Conservatives failed to win in the North West is quite astonishing — among them Sefton Central, Wirral South, Blackpool South, and Bolton West.

The dramatic disappearance of the 'Lib Dem surge' took everyone by surprise — although it would appear that the Lib Dem vote rose dramatically in some areas and fell sharply in others. Even within individual regions there were bewildering patterns. The Lib Dems unexpectedly lost in Liverpool Wavertree, but took Burnley from Labour. In Wales, they won the previously marginal seat of Ceredigion on a huge 10.6% swing from Plaid, but lost the neighbouring, previously safe seat of Montgomeryshire on a huge 13.2% swing to the Conservatives. It was only in the South West, the region in which their support is most concentrated and entrenched, that the Lib Dem vote held up in any consistent way, again frustrating the Conservatives in their pursuit of key target seats.

Task 5.1 (continued)

All this suggests that tactical voting is likely to have played a major role in this election and that, for large numbers of voters outside the core areas of Conservative support, keeping the Tories out was their key priority. Lib–Lab may not have a majority of the seats by some margin, but between them they have won over 50% of the vote.

Tactical voting did not prevent the Conservatives winning in 1987 or 1992. But in 2010 it is likely to have played a significant role.

Source: adapted from 'Tactical voting works at last' by Stuart Wilks-Heeg, 7 May 2010

(**www.opendemocracy.net/ourkingdom/stuart-wilks-heeg/tactical-voting-works-at-last**)

1 Explain the term tactical voting referred to in Source A. *(5 marks)*
2 Using Source A and your own knowledge, explain why tactical voting
   has become an important influence on how people vote. *(10 marks)*

Task 5.2

(In the style of OCR Unit F851: Contemporary Politics in the UK, Section A)

Source B: Voting preferences of women, by class

	Women AB Turnout: 39%	Women C1 Turnout: 54%	Women C2 Turnout: 67%	Women DE Turnout: 73%
Conservatives	34	39	41	29
Labour	29	28	25	45
Liberal Democrats	31	25	25	19

1 Using Source A, Source B and your own knowledge, discuss
   how far social factors are still important influences on voting behaviour. *(28 marks)*

Guidance on how to approach these tasks is provided online at **www.hodderplus.co.uk/philipallan**.

Further reading

- Survey data from Ipsos-MORI on the 'Political Triangle':
  http://tinyurl.com/35yq2zz
- The British Election Study 2010:
  http://bes2009-10.org/
- Norris, P. (2010) 'The electoral politics of the Liberal–Conservative coalition government':
  http://tinyurl.com/3xkzoau

How important is the electoral campaign?

Subscribers to dealignment theory would argue that the campaign plays a much greater role in affecting electoral behaviour now than it did during the earlier aligned era. This is largely due to the absence of socialising influences and the decline in partisanship. This chapter is primarily concerned with the features and significance of election campaigns, and all that they entail. The main theme of the debate is whether they actually make a difference to the way that people vote, or whether they consist of nothing but bluster, camouflaging the fact that the fates of the parties have already been decided in the preceding months and years.

Funding the campaign

The Political Parties, Elections and Referendums Act (PPERA) 2000 introduced a ceiling of £30,000 per seat contested. For the parties that contested all 650 parliamentary seats, that set a limit of £18.96 million in Great Britain and £540,000 in Northern Ireland. Individual seat limits depend on the number of constituents and the nature of the constituency. In 2001 spending limits ranged from £6,846 in the Western Isles to £11,957 in the Isle of Wight. The Act is also very clear about the different categories of expenditure that may be incurred by parties, and covers areas such as party political broadcasts, advertising, manifestos and transport.

Where do parties get the money from?

As a result of several scandals revolving around the issue of 'cash for questions', the Neill Committee on Standards in Public Life recommended the introduction of controls on political donations. PPERA was the result of Lord Neill's recommendations, and laid down the following requirements regarding political donations:

- Donations of more than £200 to a party or £50 to an individual can only be received from donors either registered to vote or functioning as a business in the UK. Both the Labour and Conservative parties have been accused of accepting donations from individuals who were not resident in the UK —

so-called 'non-doms'. In the light of criticism of their respective tax status, and the terms of the 2010 Constitutional Reform and Governance Act, which required all peers to be UK taxpayers, two prominent donors, Lord Paul (Labour) and Lord Ashcroft (Conservative), gave up their 'non-dom' status in spring 2010. Parties are also expected to return donations that do not stem from such sources. In July 2010, the Electoral Commission reported that the Rother Valley Conservative Party had voluntarily returned an impressible donation of £2,500 from Mr Mohammed R. Nabi, who was not a registered UK voter at the time of his donation in November 2009.

- Anonymous donations must be returned.
- All donations of more than £1,000 received by local parties must be reported to the Electoral Commission, while the national party has to report donations of more than £5,000. These figures are then made public, apart from those relating to parties in Northern Ireland.
- Any company that wishes to donate to a political party has to seek approval from its shareholders.

In spite of the PPERA, the issue of how parties receive their money has not disappeared from the headlines. In March 2006, Scotland Yard began an investigation into the alleged sale of peerages to secret and significant donors to the Labour Party — an investigation that lasted over 12 months and involved the prime minister, Tony Blair, being interviewed as a witness by police on three occasions. As part of their investigation into the alleged sale of honours, the police arrested Blair's chief fundraiser, Lord Levy, on suspicion of conspiracy to pervert the course of justice, Blair's director of government relations, Ruth Turner, businessman Sir Christopher Evans, and headteacher Des Smith. All subsequently had the charges against them dropped and no other individual faced charges related to the 'cash-for-honours' scandal.

In March 2007, Hayden Phillips published his year-long review into the state of party funding. Phillips' inquiry was commissioned by Tony Blair after allegations of 'cash-for-honours' came to light. The principal recommendations were:

- capping spending for political campaigns as well as capping individual donations, with the introduction of a £50,000 limit on donations from individuals and organisations
- creating internet-based 'supporter-subscribers' for each party — each subscriber would pay £5, which, in turn, would be matched by state funding, up to a maximum of £5 million
- increasing state funding by £25 million a year — eligible parties would receive 50p per annum per vote cast for them in the most recent general

election and 25p per vote in the most recent elections for the Scottish Parliament, Welsh Assembly and European Parliament
- cutting spending by the largest parties between elections by £20 million each

Talks over the future of party funding collapsed in December 2007, as neither the Labour nor Conservative party could agree over their reliance on the unions and large individual donors respectively.

One large loophole in the operation of the PPERA came to light in 2007, when it was revealed that a North East property developer, David Abrahams, had donated large sums of money to the Labour Party using proxy identities in order to protect his privacy. It emerged that he had used colleagues and employees to 'donate' £600,000, with the apparent knowledge of the party's then general secretary, Peter Watts. Under the terms of the Act, people donating more than £5,000 must do so in their own name.

In response to the Abrahams case, and other issues relating to the Political Parties, Elections and Referendums Act (2000), the Political Parties and Elections Act was passed in 2009. Its main stipulations were that:
- the threshold for declaring donations would rise from £5,000 to £7,500
- anyone donating or lending more than £7,500 must be resident in the UK
- all declarations to the Electoral Commission have to be accompanied by a declaration as to the source of the money
- unincorporated associations making donations of over £25,000 in a year have to reveal the source of donations to themselves of more than £7,500 (introduced to tackle the longstanding problem of 'front' organisations, such as the Midlands Industrial Council, which donate money to the Conservative Party but do not declare the names of individuals who provide the donations)

Does the amount of expenditure affect the result?

A small amount of evidence exists which suggests that money can buy you (electoral) love. In its report on the 2001 campaign, the Electoral Commission discovered that in 26 of the 29 seats that changed hands, the victorious candidate spent more than 80% of the permitted total. However, more recent data tend to disprove the importance of a large war chest at constituency level. In 2005, Lord Ashcroft gave £26,500 to the Conservative association in Bedford. Yet the party only received 880 votes and Labour retained the seat. In 2010, when Ashcroft cut his donations to constituency associations, but the party fought a more organised local campaign, the Conservatives took the seat from Labour.

One could also make a link between the huge gulf between the Conservatives' fundraising and expenditure and that of their rivals in the run-up to the 2010 election and the similar gulf in the number of seats won in the House of Commons. The Conservatives were able to raise considerably more than the other two main parties, while at the same time maintaining a huge spending gap (see Table 6.1). Having the financial capability to implement a comprehensive nationwide campaign, even months before the official start date, gives a huge political advantage.

Table 6.1 Fundraising and expenditure, 2009–10

Party	Funds raised 2009 (£m) (amount spent in brackets)	Donations (£m) (exceeding £7,500) during the 2010 general election campaign
Conservatives	41.9 (37.1)	7.3
Labour	26.7 (24.7)	5.3
Liberal Democrats	6.4 (6.6)	0.7

Should there be state funding of political parties?

A small amount of money is already provided by the state to fund parliamentary work: it is called short money (for the Commons) and Cranborne money (for the Lords). All parties with more than two MPs are also entitled to a share of a £2 million Policy Development Grant to enable them to develop long-term policies for their manifestos, deliver free election mailshots and enjoy free airtime for party political broadcasts.

The main debate over state funding of political parties is outlined in Box 6.1.

Box 6.1

Should there be state funding of political parties?

Yes

- At present the Liberal Democrats are at a disadvantage as they do not receive as much from large donors as Labour and the Conservatives. Labour also benefits enormously from its union links.
- State funding removes suspicion of large donors buying influence with a party, such as Stuart Wheeler and Lord Ashcroft in the Conservative Party, or the unions in Labour.

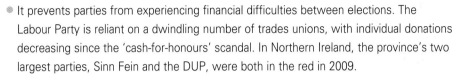

Box 6.1 (continued)

- It prevents parties from experiencing financial difficulties between elections. The Labour Party is reliant on a dwindling number of trades unions, with individual donations decreasing since the 'cash-for-honours' scandal. In Northern Ireland, the province's two largest parties, Sinn Fein and the DUP, were both in the red in 2009.
- State funding would enable parties to devote more time to political education and policy research.
- Introducing a 'matching funds' arrangement, or providing significant tax relief on small donations, would encourage parties to recruit more members and engage more people in party politics.
- Current rules for allocation of short money penalise any small party that joins the government as a junior partner. The Liberal Democrats were denied access to £1.75 million of short money after joining David Cameron's coalition, affecting their ability to plan for future elections and the referendum on the voting system.

No

- Caps on donations would destroy historic links between parties and related interest groups such as Labour and the unions.
- Taxpayers might resent their taxes being used to finance parties they oppose.
- Some opponents claim taxes could be better spent improving public services, such as hospitals.
- Any system based on parliamentary representation would make it even more difficult for minority parties to compete with the more established parties.
- Parties would expect an increase in funding from current level of income to compensate for loss of outside donations.
- As the 1994 corruption scandal in Germany and accusations levelled at several French politicians in the last decade illustrate, there is no guarantee that funding will remove corruption.

The impact of the media

Political parties try, as far as possible, to script election campaigns carefully in order to avoid unpredictable mishaps or uncomfortable encounters with members of the electorate. As a result, the only way that most voters are able to view their prospective MPs and ministers is through the media, potentially giving television, printed and electronic forms of communication a huge say in influencing the way we vote.

This section explores how far the media shape voting preferences.

The national press

The bias of the press was considerably towards the Conservatives up until 1997, when a radical realignment took place. Mirroring the transformation that was taking place on the political landscape, the press shifted its allegiance to the Labour Party, with even the *Sun* advocating a Labour victory. While this pattern remained broadly intact in 2001 and 2005, by 2010, the printed media's standpoint had changed considerably:

- newspapers backing the Conservatives: *Sun, News of the World, Express, Sunday Express, Daily Mail, Mail on Sunday, Financial Times, Daily Telegraph, Sunday Telegraph, The Times* and *Sunday Times*
- newspapers backing Labour: *Daily Mirror* and *Sunday Mirror*
- newspapers backing the Liberal Democrats: *Guardian* and *Observer*

However, did the massive endorsement of the Conservative Party have any impact on the eventual result?

In theory, the answer should be yes, as voters are less partisan and thus more susceptible to a wider range of influences. However, as Box 6.2 suggests, there are significant questions to be asked about the ability of the press to shape voters' preferences during the campaign.

Box 6.2

Did newspapers influence how we voted in the 2010 general election?

Yes

- A clear link exists between the newspaper that voters read, and the party they eventually voted for. While the national swing from Labour to Conservative was 5%, the figure among readers of the pro-Conservative *Sun* was 13.5%. Equally, the sector of the newspaper market where the gap in support was greatest, the tabloid 'mid-market', provided the largest swing from Labour to Conservative among its readers.
- Research carried out by YouGov in 2008 into the opinions of its panel of 'influential people' suggested that newspaper stories and columnists were weighted 7.3/10 and 6.9/10 respectively as to their impact on voters' attitudes.
- Long-term research has found that readers who take a pro-Labour or pro-Conservative paper for a considerable period of time are more likely to stay loyal to that party than people who do not read a newspaper.
- The impact of a newspaper's editorial position is likely to have had a greater impact on voters in marginal constituencies than those living in safe seats.

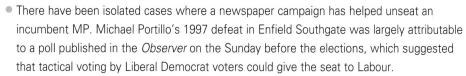

Box 6.2 (continued)

- There have been isolated cases where a newspaper campaign has helped unseat an incumbent MP. Michael Portillo's 1997 defeat in Enfield Southgate was largely attributable to a poll published in the *Observer* on the Sunday before the elections, which suggested that tactical voting by Liberal Democrat voters could give the seat to Labour.

No

- Most readers buy a paper that already reflects their own political views. The role of the press is therefore only to reinforce the attitudes of voters.
- The shift in the position of many papers in 1997, and again in 2010, may have simply resulted from a reluctance to lose readers — they simply reflected the changing attitudes of their readership. In each case, the party receiving the bulk of newspaper endorsements had enjoyed a clear lead in the opinion polls for some time. Research by Ipsos-MORI after the 2010 election found that 12.5% of *Sun* readers had already switched allegiance form Labour to the Conservatives before the paper officially endorsed David Cameron.
- The extent to which press support can boost a party's standing during the election is also questionable. The Conservatives received the support of virtually every major newspaper, yet their poll numbers fell from 41% at the start of the campaign to their actual total of 36% on 6 May.
- Equally, support for the Conservatives among readers of the *Mirror*, a pro-Labour paper, grew, with a 6.5% swing during the election.
- One of the major flaws with the argument in favour of media influence is that it cannot explain the variations in levels of support for the Liberal Democrats. No daily paper unequivocally endorsed the Liberal Democrats in 2005, yet the party won 10 more seats than 2001, and during the course of the 2010 campaign, its poll ratings improved by almost 9%, in spite of receiving only one endorsement form a daily national newspaper. The Liberal Democrats also received increased support from readers of the *Sun*, seeing the percentage of *Sun* readers voting for the party increase from 12% to 18%; yet the party's share of the vote remained constant at 23%.

Television

It has proved extremely difficult to provide any direct link between television coverage and actual voting behaviour. In the 1960s, studies dismissed the impact of television, arguing that partisan identification created a natural filter between the viewer/voter and what was being shown on the television.

In spite of this, one can identify a number of ways in which the television coverage of the 2010 campaign can be seen as significant:

Chapter 6

- With the decline in partisan identification, voters are more susceptible to other sources of information. Echo Research found that, in 2010, 85% of voters gained information on the general election, candidates and issues from television, and 47% believed it was the most trusted source of information.
- Rolling news channels provided a 24-hour feed of the politicians' campaigning. This was significant in three ways:
  - It meant that voters got to see the candidates in less favourable contexts, dealing with hostile member of the public such as Gillian Duffy.
  - It gave the parties an opportunity to control how their campaign was perceived, by allowing rolling access to stage-managed events.
  - More voters regarded television as an important source of information, and Labour had an especially poor television campaign.
- The first ever live televised leaders' debates arguably changed the entire nature of the campaign. The content of the debate, rather than the parties' spin doctors, was able to drive the agenda, allowing voters unmediated access to the leaders and their policies. In a tight election, with larger numbers of undecided voters, the impact of the debates could have been hugely significant. Research by Professor Paul Whiteley into student voting patterns found that the debates helped 40% of students decide who to vote for, and, in particular, were a major factor in moving students to vote for the Liberal Democrats.

The first of the live television debates between Nick Clegg, David Cameron and Gordon Brown in the 2010 election campaign

- However, at constituency level, television is relatively unimportant when compared to well-organised local campaigning and broader national issues. In a widely reported tweet after the first debate, Alastair Campbell neatly summed up this argument: 'election so far — first NICs, then Nick, tomorrow back to unchanged fundamentals — choice of competing futures, economy key'.
- Campbell was proved right: after reaching a peak of 31%, Liberal Democrat support fell back to 23% by 6 May.

Was 2010 an e-election?

The 2005 election campaign witnessed much greater involvement of technology than previous elections, by both parties and voters. Each party had a website, and most of the candidates in individual constituencies had one too. Overall, though, 2005 was not the breakthrough election for the internet.

The 2010 election was very different. This election was trailed extensively as the first e-election in the UK, and extensive use of the internet, and new social media in particular, by parties, politicians, bloggers and 'ordinary voters' gave this election an entirely different complexion from its predecessors (see Box 6.3).

Box 6.3

Social networking and the 2010 election campaign

Facebook
- Main source of access to the campaign for 18–24-year-olds
- Official groups established, such as the Electoral Commission's tie-in to get young people registered to vote
- Unofficial groups, such as mydavidcameron, which created and circulated spoilers of Conservative election posters

Twitter
- Real-time commentary on events, for example during the television debates
- Instant rebuttal of media stories, such as #itsnicksfault in response to stories in the *Express* and *Daily Telegraph* about Nick Clegg
- 'Academic' and partisan bloggers posted links to more detailed commentaries, such as @LSEpoliticsblog
- Gave snapshots of the campaign such as @johnprescott and his tales of touring the nation's constituencies in a Transit van
- The Labour website home page contained a 'twitterfall' from Twitter and Facebook during the third leaders' debate

Box 6.3 (continued)

YouTube

- Hosted party election broadcasts
- Conservatives bought front page of YouTube on the day of the election
- Hosted spoilers of election broadcasts

However, for all the hype surrounding the web and the election, how far did the internet impact on the campaign and voter preference? Box 6.4 addresses this question.

Box 6.4

Did the internet have a significant impact on the 2010 general election campaign?

Yes

- Young voters, in particular, used social networks to engage with the campaign. A survey carried out by Echo Research found that 42% of 18–24-year-old voters regarded social media as an important influence on their attitudes and behaviour.

- Members of Facebook's Democracy UK group downloaded 14,000 voter registration forms, and 500,000 registration forms were downloaded from the Electoral Commission's About My Vote site.

- Parties used the internet to organise and motivate their own activists. Taking their lead from Obama's pioneering web 2.0 campaign in 2008, the UK parties used Twitter and Facebook to recruit canvassers and organise phone canvassing.

- Blogs and tweets found their way into newspapers, attracting media attention in the way that a press release or political speech might have done in the days before new social media. They also acted as a rebuttal service, challenging perceived inaccuracies in the mainstream media coverage of the election. Labour activist Ellie Gellard, who writes a blog under the name 'The Stilettoed Socialist' and tweets as bevaniteellie, became the focus of media attention when she was asked to introduce the Labour Party's manifesto. The thousands of tweeters who posted to #nickcleggsfault in response to negative pieces in the right-wing press prior to the second debate were able to kill off any potential impact of these stories.

No

- Television was still regarded as the most important and most trusted source of information during the election.

Box 6.4 (continued)

- As the evidence demonstrates, social media were principally used by the younger sections of the population, but turnout among 18–24-year-olds was dwarfed by that of older voters, who did not, by and large, use the internet and new social media to access information about the election.
- The internet resembles other media in that users apply a filter to material they access. Labour voters, for example, may well have followed @iaindale on Twitter, but would have been unlikely to have been swayed by the thoughts of the prominent Conservative blogger.
- Comments by bloggers or tweeters followed stories made and broken by the 'old media' — 2010 was not an election where a story was made online; instead, it was an election where television set the agenda, and the blogosphere provided its own commentary.

Turnout

The UK is a parliamentary democracy, which allows its citizens to confer legitimacy on the government through regular elections. Elections therefore give a party a mandate to govern. If a significant minority of the population chooses not to vote at all, not only does this undermine the right of the winning party to govern, but it also raises serious questions about the legitimacy of the political system as a whole.

Turnout in 2010 was 65.1%, up 3.7% on the 2005 figure, and a marked increase on the record low of 59.4% recorded in 2001. The 65.1% national average inevitably masked large discrepancies across the regions. Turnout in Northern Ireland fell from nearly 63% to less than 58%, while the figure in the North East of England was 61.1%. Meanwhile, voters in the South East were more willing to vote, with 68.1% of them doing so.

Why has turnout fallen during recent elections?

A combination of practical and theoretical explanations can be put forward to explain the phenomenon of falling turnout in the UK. Most of the survey data suggest that a very tiny number of people are serial abstainers, while the majority of respondents in panel surveys attribute their failure to vote to practical reasons such as 'forgetting'.

The 2010 election

For many voters, practical reasons such as being too busy to vote play a major part in non-voting. In 2010, the Electoral Commission believes almost one third of the electorate did not vote for this type of circumstantial reason. This bears out survey data retrieved by MORI in 2009, which found that 'Difficulty in voting/getting to location' was the second most common explanation for dissatisfaction with the actual process of voting in the UK. A further 13% did not vote because either they were not registered, or they had not received their postal vote or polling card. According to the *Guardian*, voters from Macclesfield, Manchester Gorton, Stockport, Camden, Streatham and Hackney reported not receiving their postal votes, even though they had applied before the deadline.

Access to polling stations provided an impediment to voting for some of those actually intending to do so in 2010. Most of the election coverage while waiting for the first results of the evening on election night was concerned with the experiences of voters in locations as diverse as Hackney, Manchester and Sheffield where large numbers of people appeared unable to vote by 10 p.m. due to large queues at polling stations. The Electoral Commission estimates that approximately 1,200 would-be voters in 16 constituencies were affected.

Voters leaving a Manchester polling station on 6 May 2010

Rational choice theory

Rational choice theory assumes that individuals calculate the costs and benefits of voting, and determine whether or not it is worth their effort to turn out on election day. As far as a general election is concerned, a voter would have to see the 'point' in voting. This might exist where the voter lives in a marginal constituency, where there would clearly be an incentive to express political preference.

A comparison of turnout in marginal and safe seats also offers some support to the rational-choice argument. In the ten most marginal seats in 2010, turnout was greater than it was in the ten safest seats by almost 20%. This suggests that when voters feel that their vote 'counts' they will use it. As only 117 (18%) seats changed hands in 2010, a higher-than-normal figure, the relatively low turnout becomes easier to understand.

The stimulus effect

Another theory argues that low turnout is often the result of voters lacking a stimulus to vote. Perhaps it is self-evident that voters with a strong identification with a party are more likely to vote, but obviously parties need to reach beyond their most loyal supporters if they are to win sufficient votes to gain power. However, research from recent elections suggests that one of the principal explanations for low turnout provided by non-voters was a failure by the political parties to provide sufficient reason to vote. This was attributable to several factors:

- lack of knowledge about party platforms, and general ignorance about politics as a whole
- a perception that all the parties offered very similar policies
- general cynicism about political parties, exacerbated by the effects of the expenses scandal (although research carried out by the Electoral Commission after the 2010 election found that only 2% of respondents to their survey into non-voting cited the expenses scandal as a reason), and a pervasive feeling that the parties were simply out of touch with the needs of ordinary voters
- 18% of respondents in the Electoral Commission survey claimed that disliking parties or candidates prevented them from voting

How can falling turnout be addressed?

A number of mechanisms have been devised to arrest the trend towards declining turnout.

Postal voting

Although postal voting was already available for a small section of the electorate, such as those on holiday or in the armed forces, the restrictions on postal voting were considerably relaxed prior to the 2001 election. Between 2001 and 2010, the percentage of voters issued with a postal vote increased from 4% to 15%. Their contribution to the total turnout was significant: 5.5 million (18%) postal votes were cast in 2010. A further quarter of a million postal voters were rejected because the details on their original postal vote application did not match the details on the postal ballot.

The effect on turnout appears to have been slight, since overall turnout levels in 2010 only increased by 6% on 2001. However, the demand for a postal vote has increased in each subsequent election, and was significantly higher in certain marginal seats throughout the UK. For example, applications were up 40% in Brighton, 62% in Barnet and 61% in Edinburgh South on the 2005 figures.

e-voting

In 2002, the government unveiled an action plan, including pilot schemes, to allow an 'electronically-enabled' general election to take place after 2006. These plans, which would have included provision for voting by text and the internet in the 2006 local elections, were scrapped by the government in September 2005.

However, a pilot scheme was used for the May 2007 local elections in Rushmoor, Sheffield, Shrewsbury, South Bucks, and Swindon. The range of electronic options included:
- remote internet voting
- telephone voting
- electronic polling stations, providing a greater range of voting locations

Response to e-voting has not been favourable. After the government launched its action plan, it faced mounting criticism over its e-voting project. Concerns were expressed about the anonymity and security of voting, and even the trustworthiness of internet service providers. It has also been argued by Professor Stephen Coleman of the Oxford Internet Institute that increasing the convenience of voting will not tackle the more fundamental problems of non-voting, such as disengagement with the political process.

Even the Electoral Commission was moved to recommend that no further e-voting is undertaken until considerable work is done to improve security, reliability of voting machines and technical support.

More accessible polling stations

The vast majority of people who turned out to vote in 2005 and 2010 told Electoral Commission researchers that voting at their polling station was convenient. The main grievance about accessibility stems from disability rights groups who claim that little has been done to improve access since 2001. SCOPE's Polls Apart report into the experience of voting in 2010 found that approximately 67% of polling stations failed basic access tests, and claimed that some wheelchair users were even forced to vote on the street. As a result, SCOPE states that 35% of the respondents to its survey favour an alternative form of voting, such as online or by post.

The Electoral Commission's report into the administration of the election appears to endorse the concerns of SCOPE, as it aims to tackle the problem of the limited number of suitable buildings that can be used as polling stations as part of its agenda during the next 5 years.

Increasing voter registration

In September 2005, the Electoral Commission revealed that 3.7 million people who were eligible to vote had not registered to do so in 2005. The lack of registration was greatest among non-white ethnic groups in the UK. Whereas 6% of white people were not registered, over 17% of such ethnic minority groups didn't register. A similar number of 18–24-year-olds had also failed to do so.

By 2010, the electoral register contained 1.3 million additional entries. As expected, the proportion of the eligible population choosing to register was considerably higher in marginal constituencies, with some areas experiencing an increase in registration of 17%.

One explanation for the numbers of unregistered voters is the way that households register to vote. At present, the head of the household completes the registration, but the commission has long argued for a system of individual registration to be introduced. Under the terms of the Political Parties and Elections Act 2009, individual registration will be phased in gradually after a voluntary pilot scheme starting in July 2011. The commission believes that such a move will make it easier for local authorities to gain a more accurate picture of who is not registered, which will allow them to address the related problems of registration and turnout more effectively. Reactions to the introduction of individual voter registration in Northern Ireland have been very positive, with 63% of respondents to a survey carried out by the Committee on Standards in Public Life expressing a preference for it over the household system used in Great Britain.

Compulsory voting

Any voter in Australia, Austria, Belgium or Greece who fails to turn out on polling day can expect to be punished. In Australia, this involves a fine of A$50; in Belgium non-voters can be excluded from the electoral register for 10 years.

Currently, voting is a voluntary act in the UK, but Geoff Hoon, the former leader of the House of Commons, advocated making it compulsory. His proposal would also enable voters to tick a box for 'none of the above', maintaining the right of electors to abstain.

Opinion polls

Opinion polls have been a feature of general election campaigns since the mid-1960s. Parties rely heavily on them to gauge which messages are playing well with the electorate, media outlets use them to provide their angle on the campaign, and voters use them to plot the likely fortunes of the parties. As far as the impact on the campaign is concerned, though, their real significance lies first in their accuracy, and second in their role not just in demonstrating voter opinion, but in actually influencing it.

How accurate are opinion polls?

Having the ability to produce accurate polls is essential if polling companies are to be commissioned by agencies, parties and the media to survey public opinion. As far as election campaigns are concerned, polls have to be able to plot accurately the direction of voters during the course of the campaign and to predict the eventual result in their exit poll. Accuracy is gauged by examining the mean difference between each party's share of the exit poll and the actual election result.

Since 1970, the pollsters have, for the most part, enjoyed considerable success in predicting the winning party and the extent of support that they would receive. Polling companies allow a margin of error of +/–3%, which allows for discrepancies in the sample, postal voting and fluctuations in turnout. In 2010, the range of companies producing polls had expanded, as had the techniques used to acquire the data. This may have led to a wide range of voting predictions emerging, but, apart from odd divergences, the final (pre-exit) and exit polls were strikingly accurate in predicting the final share of the vote (see Table 6.2).

| Table 6.2 | Final opinion polls and actual result in the 2010 general election |

Poll	Conservatives (%)	Labour (%)	Liberal Democrats (%)
Harris	35	29	27
Com Res	37	28	27
ICM	36	28	26
Ipsos-MORI	36	29	27
YouGov	35	28	28
Populus	37	28	27
Opinium	35	27	26
Exit poll	36	28	27
Actual result	36	29	23

To what extent do opinion polls influence voting behaviour?

How far polls can actually influence the result of an election is open to debate. In recent elections, they could be seen to have had both a positive and a negative impact on voter behaviour.

Box 6.5

Do opinions polls have a positive impact on voter behaviour?

Yes

- Some commentators refer to a 'bandwagon effect' taking place, where voters switch their allegiance to a party that looks like it is doing well in the polls. They might do so where their 'natural' allegiance is to a minor party that is exceeding expectations, or simply because a herd mentality kicks in.
- Polls can also encourage voters to vote tactically. Each of the parties makes widespread use of local polling in order to persuade floating voters that they can make a real difference to the result. In the constituency of Cheadle, for example (which is discussed in the section on tactical voting in Chapter 5), the Liberal Democrats always make great play of the fact that local opinion polls highlight the futility of voting Labour if voters there want to prevent a Conservative candidate from winning the seat

No

- Where a result looks a foregone conclusion, opinion polls can depress turnout. This might explain why turnout was considerably lower in safe Labour seats in 1997, 2001 and 2005. In each case, the polls forecast a large Labour majority. Given that Labour's core voters among the young and less well-off are less likely to vote in the first place, knowing that their party was going to win anyway deprived them of the required stimulus to vote.
- The 'defeatist' theory of interpreting the effect of polls on voting behaviour suggests that supporters of a party likely to lose do not turn out to vote. As the evidence from 2010 indicates, turnout among Labour voters was significantly lower than among Conservative voters. Was this due in part to the party's dire showing in the polls before and during the campaign?

There are, however, several arguments which suggest that polls have a minimal impact on the way people vote:

- The possible impact of polls is diminished by the volume and strength of competing electoral information that a voter receives during the campaign. Television, the press, the internet and their own existing attitudes are all likely to have a greater impact on how voters behave in the polling booth than opinion polls.
- As outlined earlier, there are always likely to be a range of different polls presented at any one time, making it difficult for the individual voter to be influenced by any single poll. The increasing regularity with which polls appear may also make it harder for voters to identify any clear pattern to act on.
- Evidence suggests that polls tend to be viewed according to one's own opinion, thus meaning that existing voter attitudes will be more influential than the indications presented by the polls. If a poll presents an unfavourable prediction, or appears in a source that a voter regards as unreliable, then he or she is less likely to believe the poll.

Conclusion: how important was the campaign in 2010?

The campaign in 2010 was one in which nothing and everything changed. Apart from slight changes in levels of support, the campaign appears to have had very little impact on how people voted in 2010:

- The Conservatives maintained their lead throughout the campaign, starting on 38% and ending on 36%.
- Labour trailed from start to finish, starting on 31% and finishing on 29%.
- The Liberal Democrats found themselves with almost the identical number of MPs as the previous Parliament, but with their level of support rising from 19% when the election was announced on 6 April to 23% on polling day.

Yet, this was the campaign where Nick Clegg achieved his breakthrough in the first debate, the prime minister was dogged by bad luck and incompetence, and the Conservatives ran a steady but quite timid campaign which failed to persuade sufficient voters to entrust them with sole control of the government. It was the campaign of 'I agree with Nick', trending, bigotgate, Elvis impersonators, car and plane crashes, and the creation of the UK's first formal coalition since the Second World War.

So, perhaps the lack of movement in the opinion polls camouflages the impact of what was probably the most important election campaign since 1992. One way in which it is possible to highlight the importance of the campaign is by looking at the number of voters who were undecided at the start of it: in 2005, 35% of voters said that they might change their mind during the campaign, yet in 2010, this number had risen to 45%. Labour and Liberal Democrat supporters were far more prevalent among these undecided voters than Conservatives, which may partially explain the rise in support for the Liberal Democrats during the campaign, and Labour's failure to make any kind of breakthrough.

These developments may also be attributable to the importance that voters attached to the role of party leaders, which, for the first time, matched the importance that voters attached to issues. While David Cameron maintained steady, and very respectable, approval ratings, Nick Clegg's personal ratings increased dramatically, and Gordon Brown's failed to improve at all.

Overall, though, certain themes were well established even before 6 April. Brown was an unpopular leader and his cabinet compared unfavourably to Conservative counterparts in polls taken before the election. The economy was, once again, the most important issue for voters, but no party had a clear lead on the issue, and voters did not regard issues as being as important as other factors in 2010. What did come across strongly in the months before the election was the feeling that it was 'time for a change'. The Ipsos-MORI data suggested that 76% of voters either tended to agree or strongly agreed with this perspective, yet 41% disagreed that the Conservatives were ready to govern — statistics that probably accounted for the eventual result more than any of the debates or embarrassing encounters with Rochdale pensioners.

Task 6.1

(In the style of OCR Unit F581: Contemporary Politics of the UK, Section A)

1   Discuss the importance of the media during election campaigns.   *(30 marks)*

Task 6.2

(In the style of AQA Unit 1: People, Politics and Participation)

The relationship between turnout and unemployment, 2010

Constituency	Turnout in 2010 (%)	Party that won the seat in 2010	% of the economically active population of working age in the constituency claiming jobseeker's allowance (according to House of Commons Library, May 2010)
East Renfrewshire	77.3	Labour	3.5
Westmorland and Lonsdale	76.9	Liberal Democrat	1.6
Richmond Park	76.2	Conservative	2.3
Winchester	75.8	Conservative	2.2
Central Devon	75.7	Conservative	2.1
Blackley and Broughton	49.2	Labour	10.0
Glasgow North East	49.1	Labour	12.6
Birmingham, Ladywood	48.7	Labour	19.9
Leeds Central	46.0	Labour	11.4
Manchester Central	44.3	Labour	11.3

1   Use the data in the extract and your own knowledge to explain why turnout
    varies throughout the UK.   *(10 marks)*
2   'The campaign is largely insignificant in determining the result of the general
    election.' How far do you agree with this view?   *(25 marks)*

Guidance on how to approach these tasks is provided online at
www.hodderplus.co.uk/philipallan.

Further reading

- Curtice, J. (2010), 'It pays to treat the exit polls with caution', *Independent*, 6 May:
  http://tinyurl.com/353ltzy
- Gibson, R., Williamson, A. and Ward, S. (eds) (2010) 'The internet and the 2010 election: Putting the small 'p' back in politics?', The Hansard Society.
- Jones, N. (2010) *Campaign 2010*, Biteback.
- Kavanagh, D. and Cowley, P. (2010) *The British General Election of 2010*, Palgrave Macmillan.